Youth Media Matters

Youth Media Matters

Participatory Cultures and Literacies in Education

Korina M. Jocson

University of Minnesota Press
Minneapolis • London

An earlier version of chapter 1 was published as "Youth Media as Narrative Assemblage: Examining New Literacies at an Urban High School," *Pedagogies: An International Journal* 7, no. 4 (2012): 298–316. An earlier version of chapter 2 was published as "Remix Revisited: Critical Solidarity in Youth Media Arts," *E-Learning and Digital Media* 10, no. 1 (2013): 68–82. A portion of chapter 2 was published as K. M. Jocson with E. Jacobs-Fantauzzi, "Barely Audible: A Remix of Poetry and Video as Pedagogical Practice," in *Cultural Transformations: Youth and Pedagogies of Possibility,* ed. K. M. Jocson (Cambridge, Mass.: Harvard Education Press, 2013), 13–31. An earlier version of chapter 3 was published as "'Put Us on the Map': Place-Based Media Production and Critical Inquiry in CTE," *International Journal of Qualitative Studies in Education* 29, no. 10 (2016): 1269–86; copyright Taylor & Francis, available online at http://www.tandfonline.com, doi: 10.1080/09518398.2016.1192698. An earlier version of chapter 4 was published as "New Media Literacies as Social Action: The Centrality of Pedagogy in the Politics of Knowledge Production," *Curriculum Inquiry* 45, no. 1 (2015): 30–51; copyright Taylor & Francis, available online at http://www.tandfonline.com, doi: 10.1080/03626784.2014.982490. Portions of chapter 5 were published in "Critical Media Ethnography: Researching Youth Media," in *Humanizing Research: Decolonizing Qualitative Inquiry with Youth and Communities,* ed. D. Paris and M. Winn (Thousand Oaks, Calif.: Sage, 2013), 105–23. Portions of chapter 5 were previously published in K. M. Jocson with A. Carpenter, "Translocal Assemblage and the Practice of Alternative Media toward Racial Justice: A Pedagogical Perspective," *Critical Studies in Education* (2016); copyright Taylor & Francis, available online at http://www.tandfonline.com, doi: 10.1080/17508487.2016.1234493.

Published by the University of Minnesota Press
111 Third Avenue South, Suite 290
Minneapolis, MN 55401-2520
http://www.upress.umn.edu

The University of Minnesota is an equal-opportunity educator and employer.

Library of Congress Cataloging-in-Publication Data
Names: Jocson, Korina, author.
Title: Youth media matters : participatory cultures and literacies in education / Korina M. Jocson.
Description: Minneapolis : University of Minnesota Press, 2018. | Includes bibliographical references and index. |
Identifiers: LCCN 2017009425 (print) | ISBN 978-0-8166-9184-5 (hc) | ISBN 978-0-8166-9186-9 (pb)
Subjects: LCSH: Internet in education—Social aspects. | Internet and youth. | Social media. | Media literacy. | Education—Effect of technological innovations on. | BISAC: EDUCATION / Philosophy & Social Aspects. | SOCIAL SCIENCE / Media Studies.
Classification: LCC LB1044.87 .J624 2018 (print) | DDC 371.33/4468—dc23
LC record available at https://lccn.loc.gov/2017009425

For Masaya'ni

Contents

Preface and Acknowledgments

The moment I first fell in love with art making is a blur. A hobby that started out with a mediocre piece of drawing in my preteens turned into a serious study of photography and an appreciation for art-making processes. I did not know where photography would take me eventually. What I did know was that passion paired with an aesthetic eye creates good photography. A number of archived photographs became visual material for digital storytelling projects that I pursued much later in life. What I can say now is that I have been personally invested in media production and have evolved with the shifting times. I vividly remember when my interest in media production began. I was an undergraduate student majoring in ethnic studies at UC Berkeley when I first helped to produce a short film for submission in an African American studies course. It was an opportunity to explore race, ethnicity, and the underrepresentation of students of color at the university. It was a time for writing up an analysis beyond the format of a research paper; the film included a range of perspectives based on interactions and interviews with various groups of students on campus. My coproducers and I felt compelled to create something that would call attention to issues that mattered in our lives. Consistent with our academic and artistic interests, it was also a point in filmic history when media production forced us to edit our footage the conventional way (i.e., intricately splicing film and putting the pieces together during post-production). It was an exciting time for learning. More than two decades have passed since that initial production. Today, digital technology has made the editing process less grueling and more manageable through editing software such as Final Cut, Premiere Pro, and iMovie, among others.

Since my early experimentation with film, I have continued to be interested in media production, for both my own purposes and those of students I serve at the high school and college levels. I have been involved in research projects with high school teachers and students to investigate the use of digital media in the classroom. Part of my work

has been to promote literacy learning while seeking to incorporate innovative approaches that espouse new media literacies. Additionally, the
proliferation of youth media organizations has increased the number
of young people who participate in media production. I often share information with high school teachers and students about relevant organizations that surface in my research to incite ideas about possibilities
in youth media work. I also utilize various organizations' websites to
access youth-produced media to serve as models from which teachers,
students, and I can learn. YouTube, Vimeo, Snapchat, and other video
sharing platforms have been popular among youth for distributing
do-it-yourself media production. It is once again an exciting time for
learning—to understand such cultural phenomena marked by specific
histories and sociopolitical contexts. Paying attention to these developments is important in rethinking the implications of youth media for
research and practice.

A range of scholarship shaped my thinking about youth media. Individual and collective studies echo the wide interest in youth media and
also demonstrate the ongoing need for understanding an important
educational and cultural phenomenon. The perspectives on the *what*
and the *how* of literacies have been influential to theory, practice, and
research. With more advanced media technologies, as well as actions on
the part of young people in these sociopolitical times, there is a need
to further examine media production in and beyond school. What fills
these pages is an effort to illustrate specific examples of young people
producing media in supportive learning environments and, hopefully,
to further invigorate what we (can) do in the future. It is important to
make explicit the connections of youth media to curriculum and instruction, literary and media arts, and everyday participatory cultures.
It is just as important to point out that some stories embedded in youth
media reflect how young people are navigating school and society. As
they make sense of their place in the world, young people are raising
concerns about power and particularly uneven relations of power that
shape their day-to-day. They are telling stories and calling our attention to critical issues that are often not woven into the mainstream discourse. What does this mean for classrooms, schools, and other educational settings? Building on recent theories of media ecology and genres
of participation, the illustrations of youth media in relation to literacies
and spaces of possibility serve as a heuristic for supporting what young

people are already doing and what they can do with media technology to participate more fully in society. Culling together previous work in this volume, I believe, extends current thinking on youth media to capture a growing area of study toward transformative education. I am grateful for the opportunity.

Family, friends, colleagues, and mentors have guided my trajectory to complete this project. Their care and support have been tremendous. I consider myself lucky to have such kinfolk because along the way they prodded and reminded me to mark the page with love. They insisted that I eat, too, especially on the busiest days (you know who you are). To name a few, I am grateful to Erin Jasiyah Conner and Ezekiel Dixon-Román for being intellectual pillars; to Grace Carroll and Danièle Spellman for believing it can be done; to Leigh Patel, Chris Tinson, David Stovall, Cheryl Matias, Roland Sintos Coloma, Eve Tuck, Rubén Gaztambide-Fernández, Robert Simon, Danny Martinez, Elizabeth Montaño, Maisha Winn, Marcelle Haddix, and Tiffany Lee for offering a push or two; to Allan Luke, Sonia Nieto, Luis Moll, and Richard Ruiz for being exemplars; to Zeus Leonardo, Cynthia Lewis, Elizabeth Moje, Tara Goldstein, Tyrone Howard, Vivian Gadsden, Carol D. Lee, and William Trent for demanding more. There is plenty of sustenance in our conversations and I am truly moved each and every time. Just as important, I acknowledge the students, teachers, artists, producers, and youth advocates whose work continues to inspire. Some aspects of their work are represented in this book. In particular, I want to thank Chinaka Hodge, Eli Jacobs-Fantauzzi, Adriel Luis, and Karen Lum for their brilliance. It is an honor to have learned so much from them, and an even greater honor to have been able to share important lessons with my own students who then push the envelope in their own right. I also want to thank Jeff Share, Leah Lievrouw, Rhonda Hammer, Doug Kellner, Lissa Soep, Erica Halverson, Ernest Morrell, and Renee Hobbs for extending my thinking early on. Of course, special thanks to the College of Education at the University of Massachusetts Amherst for providing resources that made book writing possible; to the University of Minnesota Press for getting behind the project; and to OISE/University of Toronto, Queensland University of Technology, and University of Ottawa for propelling different exchanges on youth media culture, human rights, and education that have now come into full view.

There is a deep sense of appreciation for all who have offered kindness in different ways and made sacrifices for/with me as I darted to the finish line, particularly loved ones and a first born to whom this book is dedicated. Bringing Masaya'ni into this world has been an incredibly humbling human experience. The ground remains stable when we take the time to cherish the details. Because with that comes life's precious gifts.

Introduction
Youth Media Matters

Hues of blue and gray emanated from the screen. The room was dim. Three teens were watching a video while they hovered around a computer station, two standing up and one sitting on a chair. I couldn't quite make out the video from the opposite side of the room as I had just walked in from chatting with a colleague in the hallway. It was three o'clock on a Friday. The video seemed to be a personal project that had to be completed before the weekend, and time was short. The video project, as I discovered later, was a digital story about family and relationships. As I approached to see the screen, the video faded to black and a collective "awww" was uttered. There was a moment of peer feedback before the producer rendered the video's final edits. I was privileged to watch that version at a screening and I, too, was moved by the story. It was neither the first nor the last time. I witnessed many similar scenarios in classrooms, after-school programs, community-based organizations, libraries, film festivals, and other youth-centered spaces (face-to-face or online) that had captured my and other educators' attention. Such instances of sharing and playback reflect the power of stories.

It is no news that young people around many parts of the world are crafting stories multimodally. Because they can. Because they want to. Or because they have been asked to do so as a method of invigorating teaching and learning. Such practices not only illuminate the inextricable link between literacy, culture, and pedagogy, but also lay the ground for advancing theory in education. In this book, I take such practices as my cue for thinking anew. For example, while sociocultural theories of literacy remain central, I build on ecological and geospatial perspectives to deepen our understanding of youth media within participatory cultures (as explained in the following). I consider key markers of difference such as race, class, gender, and language to extend previous scholarship. I also discuss the notion of place as relational and the creation of translocal digital networks as vital to imagine the ways we can

1

(re)organize learning in classrooms and beyond. Old and new theories come together in this volume to examine youth media across educational settings. Put simply, the book's strength lies in the extension of theory, the microscopic lens into media making in a range of locations, and the broader purview of youth media as part of present day social and cultural movements. Youth media continues to be a hot topic and it is important to peel back the layers of what we already know to move the thinking forward.

Why Youth Media Matters

Stories persuade. Stories inspire. Stories generate ideas. With conventional and more advanced technologies, stories are produced and shared in various ways. One way is through media production. As many of us know, the media in media production can mean many things. It can refer to music, radio, newspapers, magazines, blogs, podcast, video, film, photography, animation, graphics and other visual art, and alternative mixed forms. In the case of my work with young people in the last fifteen years, media production has manifested in the form of video or multimedia composition; stories have been conceived and sometimes remixed by emerging writers, poets, filmmakers, artists, and the like. There is certainly a lot to be gained from young people who spend countless hours creating or assembling material for various purposes and in various social contexts. There is a lot to learn from young people who also distribute their videos or related types of multimedia composition using social media.

The main premise of this book is that youth media matters. It has mattered for generations, albeit using different technologies. In today's participatory cultures, youth media has the potential to teach many of us a thing or two. Youth media matters because young people care enough about something and want to share and catch our attention. Youth media matters because young people have tapped into an age-old practice of storytelling to reveal specific ways in which society structures their lives to shape the kinds of people they can or will be. Some stories bespeak weighty subjects. Some reflect the mundane. Some express absurd or frivolous moments. As an educator, I am amazed (and often blown away) by the quality of video and multimedia material available online to improve teaching and learning. I am even more amazed by the teaching and learning processes that value the transformative potential of media production in participatory cultures. Thus, it is important to take stock of a range of examples, such as videos and websites using social media, as part of networked publics (boyd 2014). The sociality embedded in networked publics has extended the ways young people connect with each other. Beyond the social, there are particular sets of cultural material that demonstrate young people's desires and penchant for crafting stories that can also inspire critical thought and action. In this book, I consider in what ways we as educators and youth advocates can continue to harness the power of stories through youth media as a form of cultural production. We shall see in the chapters that follow the intricacies of doing youth media work in a number of locations.

In recent decades, there has been a proliferation of youth media in and beyond schools. While it is not new, youth media as cultural production has marked what is possible through creativity and self-expression. It has provided producers a means to reach large (and often immediate) audiences in the movement toward social change. For many youth, it has become a palpable platform for rendering experiences often steeped in the margins. In my experience as a teacher, researcher, media producer, and classroom collaborator, I have come to know very well different sets of literacies and pedagogies that build on the interests and talents of youth who produce media that matters—not only in their lives but also in their communities. This book is an effort to bridge some of my own experiences and offer a combined perspective on literacy, digital media, and comprehensive education.

Drawing from interdisciplinary scholarship, *Youth Media Matters* highlights the purposeful collaboration between students and the teachers and other adults who work with them. Specifically, what is new here is a connective analysis of what has taken place in content area classrooms, career and technical education, literary and media arts organizations, community television stations, and colleges and universities. Findings from four separate studies offer a unique perspective on do-it-yourself (DIY) production—a kind of material, cultural, and human remix—that is key to understanding youth media. Each chapter opens up with a story to situate and humanize the studies; each story marks an entry point to a specific place or to an interaction relevant to the chapter's focus. This is intentional in order to reference right away different educational settings of which youth media was a part. My position also becomes apparent as I tell each story from a particular lens, for instance, collaborating with social studies and English teachers in California, participating at a women of color film festival, visiting a museum at a local park with a multimedia communications teacher in Missouri, trying out different classroom and library spaces to teach a university course, and touting a trending video on social media while deep in the mountains only to discover it isn't so current.

It is a joy to recount the stories. They reflect the personal and the professional and the entangled selves unraveling through relationships, with everyday textures shaping each moment. More important, the stories allude to what, where, and who constitutes youth media aside from youth themselves and the spaces they occupy. Guiding questions that influenced what is presented in this book are as follows: How do youth media shape culture, and vice versa? What types of knowledge are produced by youth and why? What is involved in the process of multimedia composition and DIY production? What literacies emerge along the way or are enhanced over time? What pedagogies and repertoires of cultural practice support youth to leverage their knowledge toward civic engagement? What can we learn from youth about the human experience in the digital age? What can educators, youth advocates, parents, and policymakers learn from youth media to rethink possibilities in education?

Most exciting about this book are the concrete examples of youth media work. Insights are drawn from studies conducted with and among youth in the San Francisco Bay Area, New York, and St. Louis. Youth represented in the book range in age (from fifteen to twenty-four years old). They are from racially, ethnically, culturally, and linguistically diverse groups, including African Americans, Chicanx, Latinx, Asian Americans, and Pacific Islanders. Many of the high school and college-aged students are from low-income families; some are from first-generation immigrant backgrounds. The majority of students in my classroom at the university are European American or White, with a small number of students of color; many are from middle-class backgrounds. While the approach is necessarily interdisciplinary, the descriptions highlighting these youths' experiences are grounded both in theory and practice specific to education. Featured are examples of youth media work such as scripts, videos, and television broadcasts; key websites and links to related examples are also included. The book comes at a time when more and more educators are attentive to participatory cultures and are seeking ways to improve teaching and learning in the digital age. Doing so supports young people in their processes of becoming; becoming more civically engaged and participating more fully in society by creating and sharing cultural material they deem important. The multiple, often connected, stories young people tell reflect a kind of knowledge production that has import both in and out of the classroom. As we shall see in the chapters, youth-produced media can raise awareness about particular cultural, social, and political issues mediated by youth's experiences. In a time of advanced technologies and increased online connectivity, the potential for building individual and societal capacities is augmented by translocal discourses and global cultural flows via media production. My task in writing this book is to provide a particular lens into how this happens.

Media Production in Participatory Cultures

Youth engage various forms of media technology in their lives. Those born after 1980 are distinct from other generations largely because of their use of technology. A study of American teens and technology showed about 73 percent with cell phones (half of those with smartphones), 23 percent with tablets, and 93 percent with access to laptop or desktop computers (Pew Research Center 2010). Similarly, a study of eight to eighteen year olds indicated increased media use per day (approximately eight hours for teens); the media include television content, music/audio, computers, and video games. A three-wave study of media use conducted by the Kaiser Family Foundation in 2009 reported that young people ages eight to eighteen spent an average of seven and a half hours a day, seven days a week, on television content, music/audio, computer, video games, print, and movies (Rideout, Foehr, and Roberts, 2010). This average implied an increase of two and a half hours a day over the past five years. With multitasking, of course, the amount of time youth use media signaled a jump to over ten hours per day.

Apart from technology and media use, continued research and practice to understand participatory cultures and networked publics point toward innovation in education (Delwiche and Henderson 2013; Jenkins 2006a, 2006b; Jenkins, Ito, and boyd 2016; Ito et al. 2013). A concern for educators and a central issue I raise in this book is how youth as media consumers *and* producers participate in and beyond classrooms. It is important to examine the interplay between what young people do with technology and the ways in which technology as dialogical tools of power can support particular forms of learning through media production across educational settings. To be clear, a participatory culture in contemporary society is defined as one:

1. with relatively low barriers to artistic expression and civic engagement
2. with strong support for creating and sharing one's creations
3. with some type of informal mentorship whereby what is known by the most experienced is passed along to novices
4. where members believe that their contributions matter
5. where members feel some degree of social connection with one another, or at least care about what other people think. (Jenkins, 2006a, 7)

It is argued that a participatory culture enables young people to "participate" through affiliations, expressions, collaborative problem-solving, and circulations. While this may be true in many cases, concerns remain about who has access to opportunities (participation gap), how media shapes young people's perceptions of the world (transparency problem), and the ability of traditional forms of professional training to prepare young people in their increasingly public roles (ethics challenge). As well, within participatory cultures, the implicit treatment of language needs to be addressed, that is, what languages are included and whose languages matter or whose do not in shaping artistic expression and civic engagement (Jocson and Rosa, 2015).

Moreover, it is true that contemporary society is part of a participatory creative and knowledge culture in which people find ways to work together to collectively classify, organize, and build information, or what has been termed "collective intelligence" (Lévy, 1997). This includes participatory economic and political cultures that mark radically different, nonmarket mechanisms in the information economy. It was not always like that. Delwiche and Henderson (2013) suggest four distinct phases of participatory culture: emergence (1985–1993), waking up the Web (1994–1998), push-button publishing (1999–2004), and ubiquitous connections (2005–2011). The phase we are in today is indicative of the expanding information and potential for creativity, civic engagement, and activism. It is pivotal to consumers and producers of media, including young people. Such thinking has implications for education, media and cultural studies, and communication. In light of rapidly changing technologies, participatory culture as an area of study remains an emergent project across disciplines.

I first conceived this book several years ago when questions about young people's media use and digital technology's role in transformative education began to surface. This book is the culmination of several studies I conducted inside high school classrooms, a close look at the work of emerging artists at the intersection of literary and media arts, and an analysis of my own teaching at the university. Each chapter offers a particular concept to illuminate youth media more clearly. Each chapter is also site-specific to help showcase youth media taking place across educational settings. It is important to point out early that youth media is presented as follows: (1) with guided instruction in the classroom, (2) young people engaging in do-it-yourself media production on their own with assistance from other youth and adults alike, and (3) young people engaging in do-it-yourself media production toward the creation of joint projects. Some of the examples and illustrations may seem a bit dated. The nature of technology is such that it is hard to keep pace. Books take longer to get published. By the time you read this, newer ideas and technologies are likely to have sprouted. However, that does not mean that the ideas and lessons learned about youth media are no longer applicable. In fact, I argue, they serve to further deepen the conversation (see Jocson, 2015a).

Youth media requires continuous (if not renewed) thinking about literacies. New information and communication technologies continue to demand new literacies. Twenty-first century technologies such as computers, smartphones, tablets, and the like not only have created different ways of interacting with others, but also have changed how individuals spend their time in particular spaces (real or virtual). The movement toward new(er) literacies marks the transformations in a post-typographic world. Within the area of literacy studies, Lankshear and Knobel (2006) point out that new literacies are inclusive of both existing and emerging forms of literacy. Similarly, Voithofer (2005) asserts the importance of keeping in mind that "new" in "new literacies" doesn't mean better or best or that one form supersedes the other. We are in a specific historical period in which production, distribution, and reception are at the forefront of participatory cultures. That is, changes in information and communication technologies beg us to ask questions about the convergence of texts (the mixing of video, photo, audio) and presentation (using particular kinds of interfaces). Of most interest to me is how youth media offers exciting ways of thinking about production, distribution, and reception in a variety of settings with young people and their work at the center to teach us about the potential of different forms of cultural production for transformative education. Thus, youth media is framed by specific illustrations of youth media as assemblage, as critical solidarity, as place-making, and as pedagogy. An outline of the book is provided below.

New Media Literacies

The conceptualization of *new media literacies* has been influenced by a number of perspectives in education, media and cultural studies, and communication. Theoretically, what constitutes new media literacies? What counts as new? How are today's media similar to or different from the "old"? Why is the plurality of literacy necessary? Practically, what do "new media literacies" look like in everyday life and how do individuals, youth especially, utilize or leverage them for different purposes? These questions have guided my teaching and research in education for several years. In my work with students, these questions have served also as a departure point for interrogating one's personal use of media technologies that typically evoke more questions about the quandaries of what it means to live in a digitally mediated world.

In examining youth media in this book, I build on my experience as a university instructor, researcher, and collaborator in high school classrooms. The terms *new, media,* and *literacies* provide a baseline for understanding and a catalyst for theory building. The plural form of the word *literacy* (literacies) is significant because we know that there are multiple ways of using language to communicate in oral, written, or other multimodal forms, as well as using multiple languages in order to do so (New London Group 1996). With this view, literacy is treated not simply as a set of neutral skills but rather as situated ideological social practices (Street 1984; 1995). Research studies on cultural ways of learning have noted the significance of repertoires of cultural practice for understanding literacies in contemporary times (Gutiérrez and Rogoff 2003; Lee 2007). Throughout this book, I use *literacy* and *literacies* interchangeably where appropriate. For me, what has become provocative over time since I began engaging in youth media work are not the shifting meanings embedded in each of the terms that constitutes *new media literacies* but the emergent thinking, and thus emerging concepts, when these terms are combined to produce three exciting areas of study: new media, new literacies, and media literacies. The breakdown of "new media literacies" into three different yet interrelated concepts is important for understanding youth media and its educative possibilities.

According to Lister et al. (2009), the new in "new media" points to change and continuity of practices that is shaped by but not reducible to technologies. The pace of change is unparalleled and, as they argue from a media and cultural studies perspective, has resulted in "new textual experiences, new ways of representing the world, new relationships between subjects and media technologies," as well as new ways of embodying identity and community and new patterns of organization, consumption, production, distribution, and use (Lister et al. 2009, 12). New media are characterized as digital, interactive, hypertextual, virtual, networked, and simulated. As we shall see in the following chapters, new media enabled the exchanges among students and other youth producers. In particular, the pace of change and continuity of practices shaping youth media is taken up in the final chapter.

Similarly, Lankshear and Knobel (2006) suggest that the new in "new literacies" is ontologically shifting everyday social practice and classroom learning. Their perspective renders two nodes of thinking relevant to education: new technical stuff (technology) and new ethos stuff (mindset). With the new technical stuff, the shift from analog to digital enables different ways of reading, writing, communicating, and sharing through various interfaces. With the new ethos stuff, the emergence of a distinctly contemporary mindset of collaboration, participation, and distributed expertise enables fluidity, openness, and hybridity. This type of mindset has implications for students and teachers who find themselves at the forefront of changing practices and changing technologies within and beyond the school walls. The "ethos" of collaboration, participation, and distributed expertise is part of what I discuss in chapters 1 and 4.

Lastly, Kellner and Share (2007) note the value of "media literacies" in education as the ubiquity of media (and its many forms) has come to dominate screens present in youth's lives. Through what they call critical media literacies, the emphasis is on the explicit deconstruction of ideology found in media forms and the questioning of power relations within media representations. Kellner and Share see this approach as one way to equip students with the ability to consume and evaluate media, including social media, and encourage civic engagement. Creative and critical media literacies aimed at forming social alliances and place-making are discussed in chapters 2 and 3, respectively.

A working definition of *new media literacies*, then, is as follows: (1) the ability to communicate using multiple modes and languages in particular contexts, inclusive of speaking/listening and reading/writing texts (broadly construed), (2) the ability to utilize media technologies toward new experiences with texts and relationships, (3) the ability to build on a mindset of collaboration, participation, and distributed expertise in classrooms and beyond, and (4) the ability to consume and evaluate media forms as well as media representations more critically in order to challenge normalized discourses toward transformative cultural production. I believe this working definition offers a common ground that coheres much of what is shared in this book. More important, theories of assemblage, critical solidarity, place-making, and pedagogy expand the thinking on youth media in relation to new media literacies.

Other relevant scholarship on digital media and learning articulates the need for understanding new media literacies in a participatory culture. Jenkins (2006a) posits that new media literacies are a set of core competencies and social skills in a new media landscape. A provisionary list of skills includes play, performance, simulation, appropriation, multitasking, judgment, distributed cognition, collective intelligence, judgment, transmedia navigation, networking, negotiation, and visualization (see www.newmedialiteracies.org). As I will point out in my work with students in the college classroom, these core competencies and social skills (with the exception of simulation) emerged as key practices toward youth cultural production and participatory politics. Moreover, Ito and colleagues (2013) offer a model of connected learning that fuses learning principles (youth's interests, peer culture, and academic achievement) with design principles (hands-on production, shared purpose, and open networks). Driving this model of connected learning are core values of equity, full participation, and social connection.

This book highlights youth media as an everyday practice in an increasingly participatory culture. Some are situated in classrooms and schools. But mainly youth media is embedded in the everyday lives of young people who are engaging media production on their own, collaborating with each other, and distributing their work to reach a wide audience. Youth media as an everyday practice is important to consider within the historical, social, cultural, economic, and political contexts that shape education. The empirical studies and the range of media examples produced across educational settings in this book offer insights into how youth explore the relationship between school and society in their lives. The examples reflect the fluidity of such experiences—not as something isolated or as a specific task that happens squarely inside or outside of school. Youth media complement a critical human geography, that is, a type of geography that treats individuals not as structurally prescribed but as active in (re)fashioning the social production of space. With this in mind, youth media can produce spaces of possibility for historically marginalized populations, including youth of color and youth from low-income backgrounds. The spaces of possibility, I argue, are very much present in the teaching, learning, and production processes where changing technologies and changing literacies are demanding renewed ways of thinking about young people's stories, their use of media and digital technology, and the manner in which they are claiming their right to speak and be heard. This book takes a step in that direction.

Audience and Outline of the Book

The book is written for students, academics, cultural workers, and partners in education (youth and adults alike) interested in youth media and cultural production. It is primarily written to spark more conversations about literacy, digital media, and comprehensive education in ways that can improve teaching and learning across educational settings. The book is also suitable for youth advocates and practitioners outside of education, including social workers and artists. With its range of examples, the book appeals to a general audience interested in youth, technology, and the cultural material produced by young people now available on social media. While studies represented in the book are U.S.-based, the perspectives I offer speak to a global audience thanks to the translocal dimensions of the studies. I believe *Youth Media Matters* has the potential to resonate with a global audience, particularly because several examples cited in the book have already been made available on YouTube or screened at international film festivals. There are many existing youth media programs in the private and public sector across the globe, and this book can add to their respective goals of connecting young people through the exchange of youth cultural production.

I have been fortunate to spend time inside many classrooms to work with students and teachers. The ideas presented here are as much theirs as mine. My professional networks via the American Educational Research Association (AERA), National Council of Teachers of English (NCTE), Literacy Research Association (LRA), and National Association for Media Literacy Education (NAMLE) have been places for building the ideas that now fill these pages. The many exchanges with young people, educators, artists, and other advocates both in and outside of the field of education have been crucial. Talking with university colleagues and scholars who are engaging multiliteracies work in Canada and Australia has extended my thinking. What I present here is in part a reflection of those exchanges.

This book blends a range of perspectives from the humanities and the social sciences. The set of concrete examples introduced in the chapters distinguishes this work from previous volumes. First, I discuss the term new media literacies and delve into youth media and shifting practices in participatory cultures to help cohere ideas presented in the chapters. The conceptualization of new media literacies is important for extending the thinking on youth media as assemblage, as critical solidarity, as place-making, and as pedagogy. The media produced and distributed by youth become resources for various types of cultural remix and learning opportunities.

Chapter 1 focuses on youth media as assemblage in content area classrooms, in this case, ninth-grade social studies. Students' projects about immigration and migration were submitted to a "Coming to California" digital storytelling contest. In part a response to current issues in literacy and urban education, the study shows the potential for building students' literacy repertoires, innovating core subject instruction, and shaping the larger culture of a newly formed small school. The school in which the study took place primarily served students from low-income, multiracial, multiethnic, bilingual or multilingual backgrounds. Analysis of the students' projects offers insights into how modality, knowledge, and convergence were integral in media production. The idea of do-it-yourself expanded to do-it-together production reflects a kind of connectedness and mindset of collaboration as afforded by digital technology.

Chapter 2 examines youth media as critical solidarity at the intersection of literary and media arts. Featured are two examples, "Slip of the Tongue" and "Barely Audible." The videos suggest a kind of cultural remix that allowed youth in specific artistic genres to work together toward a larger artistic project. The collaboration between poets/writers and producers/filmmakers was key in the multimodal design, production, and distribution. The videos are widely acclaimed and have reached a broad audience through event screenings, film festivals, personal websites, and social media sites. A close analysis of the videos suggests a variety of stylistic choices that render youth-made films not only as a product of identity, but also as a form of social critique and action. At the heart of the chapter is critical solidarity, that is, the social commitment to alliance by those who work across settings, genres, and mediums in a participatory culture.

Chapter 3 describes youth media as place-making within career and technical education. A project called "Put Us on the Map," created by students in a high school multimedia communications classroom, illuminates the connection between media production and place-based approaches in education. Students utilized geographic information systems and other mapping tools to produce op-ed segments as part of a larger project about their neighborhoods. Topics included education (school closures, graduation rates), health and public safety (parks and recreational centers, teenage pregnancy, sexually transmitted diseases), poverty and unemployment, and crime (gangs, drugs). Students' projects were broadcast through the school television network. Throughout the learning and production process, students had the opportunity to conduct critical inquiries into these topics as well as participate in a professional apprenticeship setting. The learning ecology of multimedia communications and the material ontologies of place are key in the discussion.

Chapter 4 discusses youth media as pedagogy in the context of a college classroom. A course on new media literacies facilitated particular activities and assignments such as blogging and the creation of a digital story and a social action multimedia project. Theories and practices of new media literacies guided the work in a semester-long course. Note-worthy are the ways in which the resultant social action projects (video documentaries and interactive websites) served as an example of engaging in the politics of knowledge production. What happens when participatory politics become a key component of the classroom experience? In this particular college classroom, students and I discovered that processes of becoming are an integral part of knowledge production. An ethos of collaboration, participation, and distributed expertise was shaped (and was being shaped by) our very own social and cultural experiences as learners, creators, and tinkerers. New media literacies as social action emerged as a key insight. What became evident in the course were lessons about how mediation between the human, the material, the discursive, and the digital can offer new experiences and new possibilities.

Lastly, chapter 5 considers educative possibilities of youth media in an increasingly participatory culture. The chapter pulls together ideas presented throughout this book: youth media as assemblage, youth media as critical solidarity, youth media as place-making, and youth media as pedagogy. I make explicit the translocal practices within media production. Building on the discussion in chapter 4, I share some insights from teaching a new media literacies course to highlight the ways in which cultural material can travel to incite the exchange of ideas toward the creation of alternative media in translocal digital networks. The notion of translocal assemblage is important for advancing critical education. A close look at multimedia poems that take up the topic of race, gender, and the underrepresentation of Black students at two major universities makes clear how translocal practices are further amplified by today's technologies and participatory cultures. In this final chapter, I also offer directions for research and practice of youth media in these politically austere times.

Distinct in this book are the multiple perspectives for understanding youth media. The questions that originally guided the empirical studies are shaping new questions. In what ways are youth moving from media production to other forms of social action? What cultural remixes support do-it-yourself or do-it-together production within classrooms and beyond? How are youth media shaping discourses about young people locally, nationally, and globally? The field is wide open. I hope that what emerges for the reader are the ways in which contemporary histories and advanced technologies mark a participatory politics where youth can be front and center. In the United States alone, we have seen precedents set in recent years to remind us of the power of media production as social action. The use of social media to target young voters was significant in the election of President Barack Obama, not once but twice, in 2008 and 2012. As I write this, another presidential election has occurred. It was evident that incoming president-elect Donald Trump and outgoing secretary of state Hillary Clinton were both active on social media. While the results of the election are problematic for many Americans, the way participatory politics propelled each candidate's campaign is unquestionable, inciting conversation through televised debates and town halls with hashtags such as #makeamericagreatagain and #istandwithher to further influence voters' positions.

There is much to anticipate in the years to come as race, ethnicity, gender, sexual orientation, class, religion, and citizenship (among others) take center stage and impact the everyday lives of people, including children and youth. The question now is how will young people through media and cultural production shape future forms of social action? Whose voices will be heard and how will they be heard? The time is ripe for telling more stories. The time is ripe while social and cultural movements such as #blacklivesmatter and #waterislife remain strong in the midst of political turmoil. In classrooms and beyond, young people are brainstorming, writing, producing, and sharing media that matters in their lives. They are arguably more visible and more audible than ever in the movement toward change. And they are helping us to advance our understanding of youth media and why youth media matters. It is my hope that the book goes beyond emerging technologies and lays bare the potential of youth media in transformative education.

Assemblage in Content Area Classrooms

It was spring in East Oakland, California. The annual Digital Story-telling Contest's theme had just been announced—Coming to California—and a mounting stir accumulated between Rooms 107 and 108, the ninth-grade social studies and English classrooms. Over the course of two months, the stir filled the hallways of the building and ultimately the rest of the high school grounds, newly split into three small schools. The contest's theme provided a unique opportunity for students to write, produce, edit, and share biographical stories about their family's journey to California. It was part of a multicultural studies curriculum. Ms. Gantry, a White teacher in her first year of teaching social studies, wanted to capitalize on the contest as a way to extend student learning. I had the fortune of working directly with her and Ms. Byrd, an African American teacher in her fourth year of teaching English, to further invigorate the curriculum through project-based learning and the use of digital media technology in the classroom.

This chapter describes an instantiation of new literacies at an urban high school serving students from low-income backgrounds. I wanted to know what new literacies are involved in youth media, what forms these new literacies take inside classrooms, and how these new literacies serve the needs of students. Specifically, the chapter examines media production as a way to innovate core subject instruction, to better engage students, and also in part to assist in shaping the larger culture of a newly formed small school. What follows explores Coming to California projects about migration and immigration, and how they resulted in key connections among students.

Research studies have shown the relevance of digital media technologies in youth's lives (Alvermann 2010; Davis and Merchant 2009; Ito 2010). In particular, literacy researchers have been concerned with the proliferation of spaces where young people engage different forms of technology and communicate with others using different interfaces. Today, these include but are not limited to computer desktops, laptops, mobile phones, and other devices such as iPads or tablets. For example, many users participate in various social networking sites, video games, and online fiction, and do so to be with their friends or others with shared interests (Beach 2007; Black 2008; boyd 2014; Gee 2007; Ito et al. 2013; Jenkins 2006a). With developments in theory and practice, it is important to examine youth media inside urban school contexts and the implications of digital media technology for teaching and learning (Morrell et al. 2013). Youth media is a cultural movement and an educational practice that has the potential to engage young people in creating media around their interests. I offer a particular look at new literacies, assemblage, and media production in a ninth-grade social studies class. First, I begin with several key terms to situate the discussion.

Do-It-Yourself, Do-It-Together: Assemblage

DIY and DIT Production

The nature of do-it-yourself (DIY) production common in youth media leads to learning opportunities in and out of the classroom. DIY allows creators to not only experiment but also to execute various aspects of production (i.e., shooting footage, composing, and editing) on their own. The "tasks, tools, and knowledge" involved in DIY suggest a kind of ethic that renders ordinary people capable of producing quality work in certain domains (Lankshear and Knobel, 2010). In the digital era, lacing together audio, still, and moving images is done with much more ease than in previous decades. The accessibility of technology also allows more educators to integrate DIY production in ways that further develop students' literacies and integrate media education into the curriculum (Guzzetti, Elliott, and Welsch 2010; Hobbs 2007, 2011).

In my studies, it has become apparent how DIY production turns into do-it-together (DIT) production and resembles the concept of assemblage, a term borrowed from the language of art that refers to the gathering of prefabricated materials in art creation (Waldman 1992). That is, within the process of DIY and DIT production, materials include "found objects" that are altered or combined with other found objects during the art creation process. Mass-produced and often mundane items allow for a certain manipulation of objects and a particular meaning-making process. The works of art become new(er) assemblages through a process of fitting together portions or fragments removed from everyday environments without alteration (Seitz 1961). In one well-known in-stance, American painter and sculptor Robert Rauschenberg, known for his Combines—hybrid works that are at once both a painting and a sculpture—exemplified the culling of various elements through cross-medium creations. In digital storytelling, assemblage might mean gath-ering found objects such as archived photos, sounds, and other texts to create newer works or art forms through media production.

Assemblage and Narrative in Media Production

Assemblage is nothing new. The concept of assemblage builds on the ideas of the rhizome or what Gilles Deleuze and Félix Guattari (1987) note as the creative and dynamic nature of how things become yet re-main connected to one another. The rhizome's multiple and changing dimension has neither a beginning nor an end, and is always connectible or modifiable. In digital storytelling, a producer can draw on existing or new materials, mix or braid them together at any point, and construct different states of meaning. The assemblage, then, becomes important for understanding how digital stories can later be assembled or reassem-bled by others at a different time and space. In my work with students across grade levels, I use assemblage within digital storytelling and ask students to explore the ways in which the ideas behind assemblage call attention to layers of meaning that come together through intertextu-ality, multimodality, and symbolic creativity. That is, in digital story-telling, assemblage suggests how everyday texts and stories produced by students can open up classroom conversations about the rich social and cultural landscapes in students' lives relevant to the curriculum. Assemblage becomes key in teaching and learning.

The appropriation of assemblage in my studies reveals its viability across time and genre. As I will illustrate, youth who engage in DIY and DIT production approach their work in a way similar to how amateur and established artists in the twentieth century approached the art-making process. To create a short video or digital story, for example, youth pull together (non)purposefully designed objects found in their natural set-tings to craft something new. The art-making process is reminiscent of bricolage (Levi-Strauss 1966), a method that involves being adept at building and tinkering with whatever is at hand, in other words, making do with preexisting materials from human endeavors. The art-making process is also emblematic of de Certeau's (1984) "tactics" of artfully manipulating and reappropriating cultural goods imposed by an external power. These tactics suggest a response by the consumer to repurpose meaning that dominates production through newer creations. As such, assemblages by youth place them in a cultural-historical continuum alongside artists whose works have been legitimized and popularized by culture industries, as well as those whose works have yet to be seen or recognized by the masses. Assemblages can position young people as producers of knowledge to expand larger discourses of history, culture, and politics.

Apart from assemblage in art making, another important aspect of DIY and DIT production is narrative. Derived from narrative theory, "narrative" is an abstraction of history, a congealing of experience into a chain of events that is part of a larger whole common in storytelling and conversation (Labov and Waletsky 1967). Narrative refers to recognizable daily scenes or familiar folk stories, which according to Bruner (1991) represent a construction of reality. The temporal dimension of narrative distinguishes itself from a simple list of events; rather, narrative gives precedence to individual experiences and actions in relation to their effect on the larger whole (Polkinghorne 1988). A narrative's organizational structure provides a window into human activity that results in linguistic or discursive productions, oral, written, or otherwise. Telling stories through media production takes on such characteristics, with attention to the whole and its parts. In what follows, we shall see students recounting narratives based on their own or others' experiences. The construction of narratives guided by particular curricular topics offered a unique window into their personal lives and family histories.

Together, the term "narrative assemblage" becomes useful for understanding youth media. Narrative assemblage suggests ways of making sense of social worlds, to explain and communicate human existence, to express what is significant through stories and art creations. Narrative assemblage makes possible the construction of reality largely through the use of found photographs blended with found music and scripted writing. Narrative assemblage also provides youth from diverse racial, ethnic, and linguistic backgrounds an axial landscape for cross-cultural understanding and knowledge production. In the digital era, youth media as narrative assemblage can take many forms, including digital stories, digital photo essays, music videos, documentaries, and animation. Some youth media producers interested in video as a medium have entered their works in film festivals, received critical acclaim, and garnered awards at the national and international level (Burn 2009; Halverson 2010). I delve more deeply into this with related examples discussed in chapter 2.

In content area classrooms, narrative assemblage offers a way to expand notions of multiculturalism beyond customary festivals and history months to celebrate diversity (Nieto and Bode 2012). As I will point out, narrative assemblage opens up doors for students to make connections about their everyday experiences while also positioning them as active learners and as joint knowledge producers. Positioning students in this way capitalizes on inquiry-based approaches to learning as well as critical thinking to further promote literacy development (Morrell 2004). Making media to be shared with others in school becomes a key activity that ultimately binds various social and political issues common among participants, one of which is the issue of migration and immigration. Before turning to the participants, I situate the study within new literacies to characterize multimedia composition in today's classrooms as afforded not only by technology, but by emerging participatory practices that open up possibilities for dialogue in teaching and learning.

New Literacies and Youth Media

New literacies such as DIY and DIT production that have emerged in the digital era are important to understanding youth media. Since the arrival of personal computers and the Internet, scholars have been increasingly interested in examining various aspects of the new literacies affecting youth's lives. In studying new literacies, it is essential (although a challenge for many) to keep up to date with the rapid changes that accompany more advanced designs, products, and tools hitting markets around the clock. There are multiple perspectives on new literacies that help propel the research field (Coiro et al. 2008; Leu et al. 2009). The treatment of new literacies as a social practice (Street 2003); as a new discourse (Gee 2007); as a multimodal semiotic platform (Kress 2003); as a reading comprehension question (Leu and Kinzer 2000); as an epistemological issue (Lankshear and Knobel 2006); and as occurring in and out of school settings (Hull and Schultz 2002) has been well documented.

But what constitutes new literacies, and what is new about them that makes them relevant to schools with rapidly changing demographics? According to Lankshear and Knobel (2006), new literacies have new "technical stuff" (digitality) and new "ethos stuff" (mindset) that allow users a different way of engaging with the world. The new "technical stuff" offers opportunities for greater speed and dispersion; the new "ethos stuff" mobilizes values and sensibilities that are more participatory, collaborative, and distributed in nature. New literacies, then, are distinct from the mindset that characterizes conventional literacies, which often are individuated or expert-dominated, even with the use of digital media technology. In other words, new literacies are not simply electronic or digital versions that replicate longstanding literacy practices; they constitute a varied mindset that draws on collective expertise. A treatment of youth media as narrative assemblage taking place inside urban secondary classrooms extends the dialogue on new literacies.

As noted, youth media may include but are not limited to video, music, photography, animation, blogs, games, graphics, and others. The engagement with forms of media differs from adults' for the mere fact that youth are involved. Their positionality within the social spaces they occupy shape unique purposes and interactions in their lives. Thus, youth produce cultural material about sets of experiences that may not necessarily be in the purview of adults. Youth media as a field has been around for some time (Osgerby 2004). It began to emerge in the 1960s and 1970s when handheld video and still cameras catalyzed the production of art forms as part of cultural revolutions in the United States and abroad. Youth media evolved at the tail end of the twentieth century when advances in technology allowed for more compact (less bulky), more precise, and more affordable hardware equipment than in the past. Youth media has reached the hands of many by employing a DIY approach to production, that is, without the need for formal expertise or support of an industry-like production team common in Hollywood film sets. The strength of youth media lies in its ability to shift with the times and inevitably to grow alongside its creators. As I will point out, a DIY approach becomes a participatory process with youth working collectively as a unit of production, competence, and intelligence (Lankshear and Knobel 2006; Lévy 1997). This participatory process is not limited to the use of digital technology.

Several studies have indicated the power and the potential of youth media, particularly those from historically marginalized communities in the United States (Akom, Cammarota, and Ginwright 2008; Hull and Nelson 2005; Morrell 2008; Soep and Chavez 2010). For example, Hull and Nelson illustrate the power of multimodality in the construction of identity and the representation of self in multimedia digital story-telling. They note the agentive nature of crafting the particular and the universal through the lacing of image, script, and sound (assemblage) in video production as part of an after-school program. Through a close multimodal analysis of one particular text, Hull and Nelson reveal just how semiotic relationships between the different modes provides the creator ways to express textual meaning more fully and more precisely.

In a similar yet broader argument, Morrell describes the role of youth media production as a form of critical praxis among urban youth of color participating in a university-based summer seminar. He maintains that while media consumption through newspapers and magazines is key it is also worthwhile to focus on production and distribution of new media genres such as digital video documentaries, digital photo-journalism, hip-hop music, and websites. Aligned with the work of criti-cal social theorists, Morrell also asserts that youth-produced media ar-tifacts serve as counter-narratives of reality, challenging or debunking (mis)perceptions about poor, non-White, and historically marginalized populations in various types of media. These media artifacts then enter the public realm through platforms of distribution (i.e., Internet, CDs, DVDs, videos, newsletters, posters) and ultimately have the potential to disrupt normative discourses in the media and beyond. Another such example is found in Goodman's (2003) work with youth in a community video arts program. At the center is critical literacy or the ability to read texts and understand power relations that inform them; it is embedded in the production and distribution of media artifacts that reach a larger audience.

Central to understanding youth media are the different forms and variety of ways youth create cultural products—whether at home, in school, in after-school programs, in community-based organizations, and in other educational settings. Despite current trends in youth media, much of the focus has been on nonschool settings due to (1) the prolif-eration of community-based programs and organizations with technol-ogy support, many in high-poverty areas, and (2) the dismantling of arts-based or elective programs in schools as a consequence of federal and state policies' emphasis on testing. As Moje (2009) best puts it, it is crucial for researchers to not only investigate exciting trends occurring out of school, but to also expand theories, methods, designs, and approaches in order to understand the relationship between new literacies and school learning or achievement.

A noteworthy study of a secondary English language arts media studies program by teacher-researcher David Bruce (2009) reports on the nature of video composition as complex and recursive, similar to the writing process. The study offers a model of composition that accounts for both print and video and treats the process in not linear but rather fluid and iterative stages (i.e., conceptualization, production, and evaluation). Composing becomes the melding of script, image, and sound elements (assemblage) to provide composers choices for representing or expressing their ideas. Given the context of my study in ninth-grade social studies, I wanted to know what students created in the classroom and how the multimedia products further supported their academic and literacy development in a shifting school environment.

School Context

Glen High School serves predominantly African American, Chicanx, and Latinx students. At the time of this work, Glen High was considered a "new school" with a population of approximately four hundred students as a result of the district-wide small schools movement that broke larger schools into smaller ones. Prior to the breakup, Glen High School was part of Central High, which housed approximately 1,700 students (57% African American; 34% Chicanx and Latinx; 4% Asian American; 2% Pacific Islander; and 3% other). The school was situated in a working-class community where 70 percent of the students' households earned less than $50,000, with 50 percent earning less than $35,000 and 23 percent earning less than $15,000. This community was designated a federal Enhanced Enterprise Community, a California state Enterprise Zone, and one of Oakland's Targeted Employment Areas—all indicators of urban poverty.

It was social studies teacher Ms. Gantry's first year of teaching. She was teamed up with an English teacher who had been at Glen High School for four years with the goal of engaging their students in cross-curricular projects. In the previous school year, I had the opportunity to collaborate with the same English teacher on a contest-inspired writing project with tenth-grade students. As a Filipina American researcher from a nearby university I was visibly an outsider in the school, but my role as a teacher-collaborator over time allowed me to be received as an insider and to be invited into the classrooms where I spent much of my time. I was also familiar with some of the cultural experiences described by participants given my own upbringing in an immigrant household.

Ms. Gantry was a member of a four-person core teaching team (including two White male teachers in math and science, also in their first year of teaching). Each teacher on the team had approximately twenty to twenty-five students per class. Students in Ms. Gantry's classes participated in a demographic survey and were part of participant observations conducted during a six-month period. As a representative sample, six focal students of color were selected based on teacher recommendation, consent, and availability. Three were African American students (2 identified as male, 1 female) and three Chicanx/Latinx students (2 identified as female, 1 male). These students had social studies and English classes together and had a similar course schedule throughout the day. Students' grade-point averages ranged from 3.2 to 4.0 on a 4.0 scale.

Stages of Media Production

Along with the oral, written, visual, graphic, and sonic affordances of digital media, I paid attention to three stages of media production in relation to classroom learning. I marked the stages *pre-production, in-production,* and *post-production* (Goodman 2003). Similar to Bruce's (2009) model of video composition, the stages that compartmentalize specific activities in conceptualization, production, and evaluation do not limit creators to a linear progression. The process within each stage and the interaction between them is fluid and recursive. The stages are defined as follows:

- *Pre-production* (conceptualization) generally includes brainstorming, reading, and writing that happens in class.
- *In-production* (production) generally includes stitching or braiding—that is, putting together all the elements of the collected material.

- *Post-production* (evaluation) generally includes self and peer critiquing, rendering the edited timeline to video, archiving their project-related files, and preparing for a public presentation (or another form of dissemination).

The latter stages of this process are similar to what is considered the post-production stage in most professional film or video productions. A principal difference between DIY (amateur) and studio-backed (professional) productions is that there typically is neither a crew nor a budget to assist in the process. What students did have in the social studies classroom was support, sometimes in the form of critical feedback, from peers, teachers, and adult volunteers from participating after-school programs or youth media organizations.

The narratives created in Ms. Gantry's social studies class for the Coming to California project commonly blended the personal and historical, as the work detailed in the next section illustrates. While Bruce (2009) emphasizes the importance of *process* analysis in youth media production, doing *content* analysis in the context of the Coming to California project acknowledges the diverse takes on migration and immigration based on students' experiences on the one hand, and on the other uncoils the tangled connections of personal–historical narratives to the broader social studies curriculum. Both process and content analysis provide nuanced ways to understand youth media production.

Coming to California: A Multimedia Project

Getting Started

The Coming to California project was centered in a semester-long social studies class setting out to study multicultural history during the period between World War II and the present. At the time of this work, there was a call for submissions to a digital storytelling contest sponsored by KQED, a public broadcasting network in northern California.[1] The Coming to California project was timely as it was situated within an opening unit on migration (concurrent with the examination of Japanese internment in World War II; later in the course the focus shifted to the Black Panther Party and United Farm Workers movement). There was no assigned textbook for this particular ninth-grade multicultural studies class. Instead, Ms. Gantry provided students with a variety of materials, including primary sources, newspaper articles, videos, maps, and Internet sources. For their unit project, students were asked to spend two weeks doing research using archival materials, oral history, and interviews with family members. Together, these methods offered students an opportunity to explore the topic in more precise ways. Ms. Gantry described at length what the process involved[2]:

> The first thing that students had to do was a homework assignment. There were six basic questions, like who in your family came to California? So they could pick anyone. Where did they live before coming to California [if they are not native to this land]? Why did they come? When did they come? How did they get here? And then the final question was to find some interesting thing about the journey or maybe something funny that happened or something really kind of outlandish. So that was the first step.
>
> Then they brought those homework questions back and . . . started working in class on writing . . . a script about how someone in their family came to California. So that was the second step, they had to go from the homework questions to the script. . . . The six homework questions, that was kind of to give them the foundation, and then from there we kind of just started talking about how to write the script in class and for homework.
>
> Then from there I had them do a kind of a peer review. I created a little form and they had to help each other revise the scripts and then I would meet with them and help them revise, so that was the next step. After that, we talked about storyboarding and what a storyboard was and students were then supposed to take their script and put it into a storyboard format. That was the part that was a little bit shaky. When I do this project again for first-time students, I really have to give them a much better sense of how to complete the storyboard. Because basically what ended up happening was we ran out of time. So they went straight from the script into iMovie, which is fine, but it's helpful for them I think if they have that storyboard ready to go and they know how they want to arrange everything.
>
> Moving from the storyboard [stage], they brought in pictures and scanned the pictures using Adobe Photoshop. They would

scan, crop, rotate, all that kind of stuff. They had to create a voice-over [based on their script] so they had to learn how to use Sound Studio. That's a lot now that I think about it. So they did all that stuff and then they're finally ready to start in iMovie. . . . They would import the voiceover, they would import all their pictures, and they would import any music that they had. And then they basically went to the editing process and they had to figure out how to edit the movie so that their voiceover would match with their pictures, with their images, and what kind of music to use to even out the digital story. And for those that were doing really well, they learned how to do pretty sophisticated stuff with the editing, using the transitions and the title screens and all that.

Space, Time, and Equipment

Producing a story with its various parts is no easy task. From my vantage point as a teacher-collaborator, what became evident were students' consistent negotiations with space, time, and equipment. For example, the desks and tables in Ms. Gantry's classroom were rearranged so that various stages of production could happen simultaneously. Students worked either individually, in tandem, or in groups at their designated laptop computer areas. These arrangements may seem commonplace to enable certain activities. However, such material dimensions of media production are mutually constitutive and are important in shaping what students do. Depending on the production stage, students also utilized Ms. Byrd's English classroom (Room 108) and the backroom office across the hall from Ms. Gantry's Room 107. The backroom was equipped with a desktop computer and served as a quiet environment for recording a voiceover. On several occasions, students asked permission to use another teacher's classroom down the hall when it was not in use during a conference period.

In addition to class time, students also showed up during the lunch hour and sometimes before and after school to work on their projects. Ms. Gantry noted the following:

> Ms. Byrd and I would come in early and stay late. Students were really committed to finishing, and we were committed to making

sure that they got done. I know it was a challenge for me. . . . Ms. Byrd was nice enough to switch rooms, which was a huge help. If she hadn't done that, there was no way we could have created the project. In a way it was a special time too because the hallways had traffic early in the morning and after school. I know it's only my first year [of teaching], but we started to notice a change in our small school, a little more gelling, a little more respect and trust among students. I could see the community we wanted to build growing right before my eyes.

The tools and equipment available in the classroom included computers, access to the Internet, external hard drives, flash drives, scanners, TV, VCR, and other media devices. During the pre-production stage, students accessed the desktop computers (30 total) available in Ms. Byrd's classroom for writing, researching topics, or gathering images from Internet search engines. During the in-production stage, students accessed the laptop computers (8 total) with an embedded iMovie editing program temporarily provided by a local media organization. There were instances when students utilized their own personal devices such as mobile phones and digital cameras, or even borrowed video camcorders from friends or family. Overall, the production process shaping the ecology of this classroom relied not only on the existing physical space but also on the material (equipment) and human resources (media instructors, teachers, family, students themselves) that supported the Coming to California project. This ecological makeup is important to mention here to characterize the complexity of learning and literacy spaces, which will be discussed further in chapter 3.

What Students Produced

I walked into Room 107 on a Wednesday, the day before the screening event, and Ms. Gantry gave me a nod from one corner and said, "Ready or not. It's show time!" An excited hum indicated there was more going on than met the eye. Students were milling about, moving from one laptop station to another, and hovering over multiple tables and desks with endless chatter, some with media devices in hand. I overheard one group's exchange.

"Yeah, I really like it. The part about your aunt and uncle is really good."

"That was so sweet, being apart for that long! It got me all teared up."

"Yeah, I liked yours too. The news clipping was tight."

"I think this is done. Did you create the rolling credit?"

"No, but my text is in there."

"It's easy. Just go to here (pointing to a specific area on the screen)."

"Can you show me how real quick?"

"Sure."

We were witnessing the final stage of the students' Coming to California projects, soon to be rendered from the iMovie editing software into a QuickTime video file, saved on to a flash drive, and transferred to the main computer for final archiving. Before the public screening scheduled the next day, it was crucial for students to go around and view each other's projects for critical feedback. Some students seemed at ease; others seemed nervous. I must admit that I too was eager to see the final product. Students had been hard at work for weeks putting together their scripts, images, and soundtracks. Along the way, something was changing in the larger school, a social dynamic that was unfolding before our eyes. Of course, we were so focused on completing the project that it took being present at the public screening to realize the ways in which students came together.

Thoughtful incorporation of storytelling, video production, and critical thinking simultaneously fostered traditional academic *and* new literacies in the classroom. Students used sources such as oral history, books, film, music, and the Internet. Central to their creations were different genres of writing, including biography and autobiography. The lacing of script, image, and sound resulted in the production of personal–historical narratives. A total of four different multimedia projects were produced throughout the year. The project themes were based on "Inspiration" essays and "Empathy" poems in the English classroom, and "Coming to California" stories and "Japanese Internment" research reports in the social studies classroom. These narrative assemblages challenged mainstream curricula and disrupted the normative discourse related to students' school and life experiences.

The Coming to California projects, in particular, grouped student work by geographic location that drew on students' backgrounds and family histories. Content analysis showed that approximately two-thirds of the stories were about migration from Mexico and Central America. The remaining stories were about migration from the South, Midwest, and Northeast of the United States with roots tracing back to Africa and the Caribbean, and also from the Pacific Islands and Southeast Asia. Figure 1 provides an overview of forty-six student projects and shows the range of stories produced by two social studies classes. The number in the first column indicates the order in which the project appeared on the final DVD that Ms. Gantry and I put together as a master copy to be played at the culminating public screening event. Duplicate copies of the DVD were also made for students to take home. Upon a closer look, thirty-two of the projects ranged between one to three minutes in length, with eight just short of one minute.

All of the narratives were either about the students' parents or grandparents, with the exception of three that traced familial roots a generation further to students' great grandparents. All forty-six projects revealed *when, why,* and *how* their families migrated to California. Noted were specific modes of transportation—by foot, by car, by bus, by train, or by plane—as well as the various reasons for migrating. Some of the reasons shared were to join family members, to have a better life, to escape war, and to find better jobs and other opportunities. Consistent throughout the projects was the careful organization of images, selection of music, and inclusion of text and other graphics to complement the voice narration.

Many of the titles hint about who or what is featured in the project. Three of the projects remained untitled; one, number 14, was entirely done in the Spanish language; and number 13 was a tribute to "Abel," with "X" as stand-in for surnames deleted for privacy. The project entitled "Man with a Past," by an African American student named Erica, received the Digital Storytelling Contest's audience award that year. It is a multimedia project about Erica's great-grandfather and his journey from Kansas to California. It stood out because of the peculiar events described in the narrative, a palpable response to Ms. Gantry's instructions to find out "some interesting thing" that happened in the journey.

Highlights in the project are the inclusion of family photographs, an unnamed blues guitar song (instrumental only), and an actual news clipping featuring the "man with the past," who in real life made headlines and was wanted by law enforcement agencies in different states. The backstory includes a Black man, who was a victim of a racial incident that ended in him shooting a White man in self-defense. The "man with a past" lived to tell the story. For this Coming to California project, multiple

#	TITLE OF PROJECT	COUNTRY
1	My Mother Coming to California	Mexico
2	My Grandma Coming to California	Tonga
3	Uncle William's Journey to California	U.S. (Louisiana)
4	Destined to be in California	Tonga
5	From Mex to Cali	Mexico
6	Santiago	Mexico
7	Louisiana to California	U.S. (Louisiana)
8	Finally Settling in California	Mexico
9	Coming to California	U.S. (Oklahoma)
10	Coming to California	U.S. (Texas)
11	My Dad's Story	Mexico
12	From Laos to California	Laos
13	Abel X	Mexico
14	Llegando de Mexico	Mexico
15	A Change Isn't a Bad Thing	U.S. (Texas)
16	A Long and Amazing Trip	Mexico
17	Thanks to My Dad	Mexico
18	Chasing Our Dreams!!!	Mexico
19	Coming to CA	El Salvador
20	My Dad's Journey	Mexico
21	Man with a Past	U.S. (Kansas)
22	My Journey to CA	U.S. (New York)
23	Beautiful	Nigeria

FIGURE 1. *Overview of Student Projects*

modes were carefully laced together to form a narrative assemblage using various transition effects (fade in and out, cross dissolve, etc.) in the iMovie editing program.

Another example is number 18, "Chasing Our Dreams," by a Chicana student named Joana. She told about her grandparents who came from Zacatecas, Mexico, and the life that unfolded for the family across four generations. Beginning with her great-grandmother, Joana portrayed

#	TITLE OF PROJECT	COUNTRY
24	My Dad	Mexico
25	A Poor Man	Mexico
26	Gloria and the First Time in California	Mexico
27	Our Journey	Mexico
28	Coming to California	U.S. (Texas)
29	A Journey	Mexico
30	How My Mom Came to California	Mexico
31	My Grandma's Story	Mexico
32	Coming 2 Cali	U.S. (Arkansas)
33	Coming 2 Cali: A Journey Ahead of Us	U.S. (Louisiana)
34	From Louisiana to Cali	U.S. (Louisiana)
35	My Grandparents' Life	Mexico
36	Coming to Cali	U.S. (Arkansas)
37	A Journey to Cali	Mexico
38	My Dad	Mexico
39	Life's Journey	U.S. (Michigan)
40	My Familia	Mexico
41	Coming to America	Mexico
42	A California Story	Mexico
43	(Untitled)	Mexico
44	The American Dream	Mexico
45	(Untitled)	Mexico
46	(Untitled)	U.S. (Maryland)

the development of relationships between family members and the effects of migration on these relationships over time. She also mentioned struggles with work, school, and the English language as part of the experience. In the end, she located herself in the narrative by referring to an uncle who pushes her to persevere in pursuit of "becoming a pediatrician." Laced throughout were family portraits, including her grandmother, grandfather, mother, father, herself, and her siblings. Similar to Erica's narrative assemblage, the discoloration, creases, and blurred edges of several photographs indicate the intentionality of finding such treasured material to include in Joana's multimedia project. Each photograph had to be scanned and imported into the iMovie editing program. Additionally, text and other graphics were inserted into the edited timeline using effects, color, and font style; the instrumental theme song from the 1997 blockbuster movie *Titanic*, "My Heart Will Go On," served as background music (see Figure 2 for a sample analysis).

In this classroom, fair use and copyright issues were discussed to impress upon students the ability of creators to appropriate material such as images and songs for educational purposes (Center for Social Media 2007). Students became aware that remixing cultural material is a responsibility that could take many forms in and out of the classroom. Noteworthy are specific dimensions of narrative assemblage not just as affording layers of meaning through various modes in individual projects, but also as linking each multimedia project into a collective experience relevant to students' lives. The similarities and differences in their collective experience provided an axial landscape for learning about each other. It also enabled a relationship with digital media technology for advancing new literacies through collaboration and knowledge sharing. Elsewhere, I have noted the role of symbolic creativities and the art of everyday life as influential in adolescent writing and multimedia composition (Jocson 2010). Of importance in this case is how narrative assemblage affirmed students' experiences and demonstrated for them how their stories are connected to further inform their very own multicultural studies class.

Both Erica and Joana used (non)purposefully designed objects, including found objects like photographs and even commercial music, to be tinkered as a new production. The assemblage is indicative of a DIY and DIT art-making process that gives the consumer, and in this case also the creator and producer, the ability to repurpose meaning in previous productions imposed by an external power. Like "Man with a Past" and "Chasing Our Dreams," each Coming to California project with its unique representations of family and migration provided important histories that are often overlooked or omitted in the mainstream curriculum. At the same time, there were some research challenges linked to digital and visual identification that led to decisions to only partially report the projects' contents (see the discussion on critical media ethnography in chapter 5).

"Nobody Ever Talks about That": Crossing Cultural Borders

Upon completion of their projects, students noted gaining more from the learning process than what they had initially anticipated. In a group reflection, twelve students representing both social studies classes conveyed what they liked the most about the Coming to California project:

- Finding out about our family history
- Using new technology
- Expressing our experiences in a digital story
- Hearing our classmates share their stories
- Learning about other people, not just about ourselves

All of the students agreed that taken as a whole the Coming to California project offered a different approach to explore their own family history, to understand their peers' experiences, and to further examine multicultural history in meaningful ways (Banks and Banks 2010; Nieto 2002; Nieto and Bode 2012).

The project provided opportunities to use traditional and digital media technology combined with a mindset of collaboration. One African American male student said, "I was inspired to find out more about my family. I learned so many things . . . things I never knew before." A Pacific Islander female student added, "It's not something we talk about all the time but we know it deep inside." Relatedly, a Chicanx male student noted the following to emphasize the value of sharing their stories through a medium that laced together script, image, and sound:

> It doesn't matter where you come from or what you look like. The [Coming to California] project shows that it's about respecting

TIME	SCRIPT	IMAGE	SOUND
	oral | written dimension	visual | graphic dimension	sonic dimension
0:00		Title: "Chasing Our Dreams!!!" Joana ___ [effect: unscrambling, falling from top, centered] [transition: cut]	Song: Titanic's "My Heart Will Go On" (instrumental) [effect: fade in]
0:03	Voice Narration: My great-grandmother decided to come to California in the year of 1956.Her name's ___. She came from Zacatecas, Mexico. She was searching for the American Dream, to find a better life.	Photo: Portrait of aged woman and child [transition: circle open]	. . .
0:16	She crossed the border in a trailer full of people she didn't know, but she trusted that they knew the way. It took them some time to arrive but when she got here she was happy that she made it.	Photo: Long dirt road with mountains in the background [transition: fade to black]	. . .
[ ]	[ ]	[ ]	[ ]
1:18	[ ] . . . the youngest decided he had come to California to live a dream he couldn't live out in Mexico. He started working for himself. He was the only one to graduate high school and get a career. He went to college and graduated with a degree as a psychologist. Now he encourages me not to let my dream go of becoming a pediatrician.	Photo: Portrait of man [transition: cross blur]	. . .

TIME	SCRIPT	IMAGE	SOUND
	oral | written dimension	visual | graphic dimension	sonic dimension
1:38	Because our family crossed the border for a reason, and that is to make sure that we always had a future ahead of us.	Title: "Grandparents, Thank You for caring so much to give us a better future!!!" [effect: centered] [transition: cross dissolve]	...
[]	[]	[]	[]
1:56	[] ... After all what my grandparents went through, I love them very much.	Photo: Portrait of man and woman dancing (duplicate) [transition: cut]	...
2:04		Title: "I LOVE YOU GRANDPARENTS!!!!" [effect: centered] [transition: fade in]	...
2:10		Title: "THE END" [effect: centered] [transition: fade to black]	... [effect: fade out]

FIGURE 2. *"Chasing Our Dreams" (#18) Sample Analysis*

each other, asking each other questions, and being open to who we are. We all came together on this one topic. For me, it was about speaking the truth.

Coming together through the Coming to California project provided a unique opportunity for students to tell biographical and familial stories. The project was a learning moment; it was also a moment that opened up doors for connections among disparate groups at the high school and in the community. As an educator interested in urban schooling, I believe that a learning moment such as this can teach the rest of us lessons that will help invigorate the curriculum and create opportunities for civic engagement in our classrooms.

The multimodal semiotic platform (Kress 2003) with more precise representations of textual meaning became key in the interactions. Each of the multimedia projects provided entry points for beginning conversations about interethnic and interracial histories in the United States. In our general observations, Ms. Gantry and I noticed that the projects brought students in that ninth-grade cohort closer together to form a basis of mutual respect both in the classroom and on the larger school grounds. The school had been rife with tension among various racial groups and this was an instance when students from Ms. Gantry's class began to break down that tension. Ms. Gantry stated, "I don't really know how to describe it. The change was happening and students just were laughing more and interacting in a way I hadn't seen before."

Through a close reading of scripts and multiple reviews of the videos, I found that each of the students' stories shared similar experiences that would probably have remained unrecognized if not for inquiry-based projects like Coming to California. These experiences presented in a multimedia format established an unexpected yet important common ground. The participatory process in the production also led to a recognition of students' collective knowledge as part of their inquiry. A Chicanx female student named Esther, who at the end of the school year was a panelist in a Youth Media Salon sponsored by the National Alliance for Media Arts and Culture (NAMAC), reflected on what she deemed significant about the Coming to California project. In an interview, Esther offered the following about the public screening held at the Oakland Museum and the Youth Media Salon held in San Francisco:

> It was a really great experience because there were people that I
> used to hang out with every day, even people I have known for like
> my whole life, and we had to do this story about how somebody
> in our family got to California, and nobody ever talks about that,
> you know. Nobody ever says, "Oh, you know what, my mom or dad
> had to go through this to get me to where I am." And so [at the
> museum and NAMAC], you know, everybody was just having a
> good time and then some got really emotional, people started cry-
> ing and all of a sudden, "Oh My God, you've been my friend this
> whole time, ever since I was born, and I never knew that about
> you." I think it's a good experience to just let people know what
> you have to go through sometimes, or every day, to be where you

are at right now, or what you have to go through to get you where you want to go.

Esther's comments capture some of the affordances in youth media and narrative assemblage. One key aspect is how the multimodal semiotic platform can provide tools for meaning-making in more expressive ways. Esther points out the importance of family and the connections between families because they are relevant in students' lives and, as she put it, "nobody ever talks about that." The Coming to California project exposed untold stories about migration and immigration through voice narration and pictorial sequence that are often constrained by traditional forms of writing. The power of textual meaning is located in its multimodal representation (Hull and Nelson, 2005). Thus, the Coming to California project not only opened up dialogue among students through assemblage but also signaled a communal space for learning enhanced by digital technology and a mindset of collaboration. This communal space opened up a rare forum for recognizing the experiences of racialized and marginalized groups in the United States. It provided an opportunity to listen and tell about the tenacity needed to negotiate new cultural terrains. Specific illustrations of migration and immigration, inclusive of "crossing borders" (real or imagined) and naming survival strategies in a new host society revealed students' individual and collective histories and set up a stage for cross-cultural understanding.

Additionally, students' multimedia projects disrupted dominant narratives and media portrayals of immigrants as liabilities to the U.S. economy. Very apparent in the projects were the extreme hardships in doing menial labor or holding multiple low-paying jobs to support families. The projects emphasized "opportunity" in the sense of making ends meet by any and all means and, contrary to common belief, contributing to the robustness of the U.S. economy. Included in the projects featuring Mexico were vivid descriptions of the extensive journey, some with references to *coyotes* (transport guides) and *la migra* (border patrol). Projects featuring other countries or U.S. regions depicted similar themes about the nature of diaspora and its effects on the family, work, and social lives of those involved. There were mentions of caravans traversing treacherous deserts and oceanic flights reaching ports of entry like San Francisco. Noteworthy in the stories were the various push and pull factors of migration and immigration. Individuals joined family members who had left previously or entire families moved to reestablish life in a new environment.

A common thread among the stories was the volume of courage it took to uproot and seek opportunity elsewhere for the betterment of one's life and one's family. This has been the trope of U.S. history in recognition of different waves of immigrants over time, a complex settler–colonial history as Indigenous peoples and communities meanwhile continue to struggle for land rights and sovereignty. Noteworthy in the present moment is how such tropes have waned in value and targeted with dissonance certain populations, as evidenced by recurring anti-immigrant initiatives by conservative groups. In this particular social studies classroom, youth media in the form of Coming to California multimedia projects illuminates the significance of narrative assemblage in teaching and learning.

Modality, Knowledge, and Convergence

The incorporation of youth media production into the social studies curriculum opened up pedagogical possibilities. The reification, or what I have termed narrative assemblage, was made possible by *modality* and *knowledge* supported by the iterative stages of production described earlier. It is worthwhile to make explicit the links to student projects:

- *Modality* refers to the oral, written, visual, graphic, and sonic dimensions present in the production. To achieve this in the social studies class, students engaged several curriculum-based tasks such as conducting interviews with family members, collecting photos from family albums, documenting significant life events in script or image form, selecting appropriate music, dialoguing with Ms. Gantry and other students, consulting curricular texts, and researching online for relevant information. The gathered material served as fodder for the art-making process and was ultimately laced together in an edited timeline.
- *Knowledge* refers to the construction of multiple inquiry-based narratives that together formed a larger narrative about multicultural history. In the social studies class, students drew on their collective expertise or distributed knowledge about the topic of migration and immigration as grounds for dialogue.

The sharing that took place impressed upon students the commonalities across the represented groups in school and in the community.

In addition to *modality* and *knowledge*, narrative assemblage was also made possible by *convergence*. The narratives about students' families and their migration from different parts of the world converged into one place—physically and symbolically. On the one hand, narrative assemblage asserts the importance of sharing histories and cultures—for building literacies and cross-cultural understandings among otherwise disparate groups in school. On the other, narrative assemblage underscores the role of digital media technologies to help creators organize, meld, and manipulate existing texts to create new ones.

It was tactical for students in the social studies class to make do with prefabricated materials for their own interest and cultural productions (de Certeau 1984). Taking oral histories provided by family members, synthesizing them into a scripted narration, and then pairing them up with found objects such as photographs, news clippings, and music provided students a dynamic way to document a significant part of their lives. They were allowed to divert from traditional forms of writing such as an essay or a book report. Instead, the multimedia project offered an exploratory canvas on which image, script, and sound came alive. Although the duration of each project was no more than three minutes, the content captured the intricacies of leaving behind the familiar to seek a new life elsewhere. For many of the students' families, the journey to California was mired in contradictions. The persistence it took to pursue a new life was more than a success story to be told. It represented the will of diasporic peoples and the belief in new possibilities.

In addition to multiple modes, the three stages of production also point to new literacies in narrative assemblage. The process of composing a multimedia project is recursive and parallels traditional writing (Bruce 2009). It involves the careful selection of texts (i.e., image, sound, script) and lacing them all together using appropriate software programs. The authoring, storying, and editing practices suggest that students are taking on learner identities as creators, producers, and curators (Potter 2012). The use of digital media technology as well as a mindset of collaboration merged in the social studies classroom to offer opportunities for advancing new literacies (Lankshear and Knobel

2006). Within this process, Ms. Gantry pointed out some of the embedded skills essential to the project:

> My sense is that this kind of project really drew in students because they got to tell their stories, their own family stories. And then, there's just so much more that comes with it, like they learn critical thinking skills and how to manipulate all these different types of technology. So they're learning a lot, and at the same time I think they enjoy it more. And it kind of tricks them into writing because they think like, "Oh, I don't have to write." But yeah, you do, you had to write. For the Coming to California piece, they had to write a script. It's like writing an essay but there's a greater sense of enjoyment because in the end they got to make a video using digital tools. For some of them, it kind of made it more interesting.

Indeed, what narrative assemblage suggests is the importance of youth media for creating more inclusive multicultural learning environments attentive to what students bring into the classroom, however different those experiences and their contingencies may be. It also affirms the importance of representing youth voices in teaching and learning; how youth can communicate with each other across multimedia platforms; and how youth contribute to the creation of youth-driven spaces, or "youthtopias" (Akom, Cammarota, and Ginwright 2008), where their work foregrounds social difference and confronts uneven relations of power. In other words, narrative assemblage has the potential to expand larger discourses of history, culture, and politics with young people positioned as engaged citizens and producers of knowledge. There are different ways to build on narrative assemblage applicable to many other contexts. This is what I walked away with from my early studies of digital media in content area classrooms.[3]

Now What?

Youth media as a growing field presents some pedagogical possibilities to improve teaching and learning. Teachers in collaboration with youth advocates and other educators play an integral role in creating the conditions to further invigorate their curriculum. The following are some considerations:

1. Youth media can support teaching and learning in content area classrooms. It blends traditional and new literacies that engage students in meaningful ways;
2. Youth media can be a means to enhance existing literacies. Lacing together image, sound, and script requires literate repertoires, including the manipulation of appropriate software programs and advanced technologies that allow for DIY and DIT production;
3. Youth media can be a means for examining complex experiences and histories that position students as active producers of knowledge;
4. Youth media can be a catalyst for beginning conversations about difficult topics that have the potential to build cross-cultural understanding or perhaps even sort out existing tensions between different social groups.

As such, we ought to deepen our thinking about youth media and extend our own classroom practices (Moje 2009; Richmond, Robinson, and Sachs-Israel 2008). It is important to pay attention to (1) affordances and constraints in communication and representation of students' personal histories, (2) teaching and learning with digital media technologies in line with common core standards, and (3) spaces of possibility toward civic engagement in schools, communities, and the larger society. The discussion on youth media as assemblage in this chapter provides an instantiation inside a particular content area classroom. The next chapter takes us to youth media as critical solidarity at the intersection of literary and media arts.

2

Critical Solidarity in Literary and Media Arts

Opening night of the Women of Color Film Festival at the Berkeley Art Museum and Pacific Film Archive. It was a little breezy and the sun was setting behind some eucalyptus trees. My heart was racing. As I walked across the university campus and approached the building, I became more anxious as I thought about what audience members might be asking at the conclusion of the screening. Lucky me, I was one of four artists there in person for the question-and-answer session. I had produced a two-minute poetic video called "Her Ways" as an exploration of self-as-becoming juxtaposed against the changing neighborhood of Filipinotown in Los Angeles. Among the other artists was a high school student whose five-minute video about challenging standards of beauty captured my attention, and that of many others. What I had been examining in my research on digital media was staring me right in the eye. I was in the company of filmmaker and producer Karen Lum, who at the time was in high school. Little did I know that I would go on to follow her work and learn so much from the different ways it reached audiences. The film festival ended, but our conversation continued.

This chapter focuses on the work of youth media producers whose experiences and talents coalesce to build a critical solidarity, highlighting two examples across genre practices of spoken word poetry and filmmaking. Ferguson's (2001) treatment of critical solidarity—or the social commitment to alliance—offers a frame to understand youth media. It is not a surprise that DIY to DIT production has become commonplace among youth with more access to technology at home, in school, or in community-based organizations (Guzzetti, Elliott, and Welsch 2010; Kafai and Peppler 2011; Knobel and Lankshear 2010). As noted in the previous chapter, DIY to DIT production considers the role of information and communication technologies and how these technologies intersect with literacy in youths' lives. Current directions in digital media and learning research consider hands-on production along with shared purpose and open networks as design principles central to connected learning (Ito et al. 2013).

My interest in young people producing media is guided by their efforts to leverage technology and literacy as part of a dynamic youth culture. There is a growing interest in youth culture and the lives of youth of color to advance existing paradigms and practices in education (Akom, Cammarota, and Ginwright 2008; Patel 2013; Tuck and Yang 2014; Winn 2011; Wortham 2011). This chapter reflects a similar approach to understanding youth culture, particularly in interactions with different forms of media and uses of digital media technology to make sense of their social worlds. As I have learned over the years, keeping up with fast-changing technologies in youths' lives is a daunting task. What I share here are some insights into youth media and how a kind of cultural and material remix allowed youth in specific artistic genres to work together toward a larger artistic project. I begin with a look at youth media taking place at the intersection of literary arts and media arts. Then, I discuss remix and multimodality, followed by a description of exemplary videos to offer instances of critical solidarity among youth.

In analyzing the videos as text and in participant interviews, critical solidarity surfaced as a purposeful collaboration between writers/poets and producers/filmmakers whose combined interests and talents led to the creation of critically acclaimed video poems. The collaboration between writers/poets and producers/filmmakers was key in the multimodal design, production, and distribution of video poems that reached a worldwide audience through event screenings, film festivals, personal websites, and social media sites. A close look at each video poem suggests a variety of stylistic choices that render youth-made films not only as a product of identity, but also as a form of social critique and action (note: the reader may access "Slip of the Tongue" and "Barely Audible" on YouTube; viewing them beforehand may be helpful to grasp the extent of the discussion).[1] Finally, I point out practical implications of critical solidarity for educators and youth advocates in the literary and media arts world.

The following take on youth media is a result of various interactions with individual artists and field observations across physical and online contexts. My discursive entry into youth media at the intersection of literary and media arts was sparked by the work of artists I had the fortune to get to know through my earlier research on youth poetry in northern

California (Jocson 2008). Several youth at the time of my study also participated in community-based organizations such as Youth Speaks and Youth Radio—as writers and producers, as interns, or as peer mentors. These social spaces allowed for a dynamic interaction among youth with shared interests and adults who supported them.

As an extension of my earlier work, I built on poetry as a popular medium of artistic expression (inclusive of performing, visual, and literary arts). Two questions guided my investigation: (1) what types of media texts are produced and distributed by youth, and (2) what do media texts suggest about youth culture in the digital age? If young people's use of media averages more than seven hours a day, then it is important to understand the ways they are participating in and responding to media culture using digital media technology. Such actions involve more than politics and require particular sets of knowledge and literacies. Examining what young people create and share with broad audiences at the intersection of literary and media arts can offer ways of rethinking the centrality of pedagogy across educational settings.

Emerging Practices in a (Re)Emerging Field

Youth media played a role in the social movements and cultural revolutions of the 1960s. Handheld cameras in video production, photography, and visual arts were indicative of the times. Early technological advancements in the nineteenth century and avant-garde art that sought new ways of thinking in the twentieth century led to the development of media arts in the twenty-first century (Manovich 2000). Youth media, in particular, (re)emerged with greater accessibility in the 1990s and blurred the previously held boundaries between amateurs and professionals (Coryat and Goodman 2004; Osgerby 2004). The pace of technological change has shaped who can produce media, and with whom, independent of corporate media.

One affordance of digitality is clicking a button in a hypertext environment and instantaneously connecting with others around the world. In hopes of understanding independent media early in my study, I interviewed Oakland-based rapper and hip-hop entrepreneur Tajai of Hieroglyphics about digital tools in music production and the science of sustaining a business in the digital era. Tajai began his career as a hip-hop artist while still in high school. In the interview, he shared that music production is quite different from when he started in the 1990s. He discussed his ability to lay down tracks, make music, and complete a whole album based in California "with producers all the way in Norway"—that is, *without* a single physical encounter or actual time in the same studio. All of their communications for creative and administrative purposes, he added, are channeled through mobile devices, computer programs, and other digital production equipment.

Additionally, Tajai noted the significant shift from conventional to online forms of music distribution, expanding music stores to include iTunes and tapping into resources such as Independent Online Distribution Alliance (which merged with The Orchard in 2012) for boosting his music label's marketing power. This type of distribution has allowed Hieroglyphics' independent business over the years to reach unprecedented heights. Another example is a duo group called Foreign Exchange that illustrates a similar development. Foreign Exchange consists of a rapper and a producer who initially communicated via instant messaging and completed an album from different geographic points (Holland and the United States). The group's strategic start online exemplifies the opportunities made possible by digital music production. Musical genres merge as well: millions of albums blending the sounds of hip-hop, jazz, R and B, and electronica have been sold worldwide. I mention these developments in music production to suggest complementary practices in video production.

For artists in various genres, including video and multimedia composition, what this means is the potential of autonomous creators and everyday consumers not only to use digital media tools in strategic ways but also to build on collective expertise toward new forms of cultural production. Running viral marketing through social media sites, uploading videos on YouTube, and developing personal websites affords artists unprecedented exposure and popularity unconstrained by mediating forces like big media companies. In short, today's media technologies have endowed artists with nonlinearity, connectivity, autonomy, and audience that recast for many youth what it takes to create and distribute media products, and with whom they do their work. Media arts education, including the increasing attention to graphics and game design, raises questions about the potential of media making and arts learning in schools and informal settings (Peppler 2010, 2014).

Around the early 2000s, youth media organizations proliferated in

American cities small, medium, and large. According to the National Alliance for Media Arts and Culture's youth media initiative (2003), there were over two hundred youth media organizations across the United States that varied in type, size, focus, genre(s) of interest, populations served, and sources and amounts of funding.[2] Many of the organizations served youth from low-income families and were funded by local, state, and federal agencies. In the category of youth producing media, NAMAC's report indicated three major genres of interest in video production: documentary, narrative/fiction, and experimental.

In working with students and teachers interested in youth media as a classroom practice, I have found it important to consider youth media organizations, as they have increasingly played an integral role in supporting DIY to DIT production in schools. According to Coryat and Goodman (2004), youth media helps educators continue to build capacity, develop curriculum, and establish professionalism in the field. Advocates of youth, educators, and researchers have the potential to work together to share relevant resources. In "From New Media to Critical Media Literacies" (Jocson and Share 2012), I noted the collaborative possibilities of supporting youth literacy development through media literacy education. Among youth media organizations that reflect this work are the Bay Area Video Coalition and Conscious Youth Media Crew (in San Francisco), Reach LA (in Los Angeles), Street-Level Youth Media (in Chicago), and Educational Video Center (in New York).[3] Organizations and related programs outside the United States such as Asian Media Access, Young Media Australia of the Australian Council on Children and the Media, Canada's Media Awareness Network (now MediaSmarts), Mideast Youth (now Majal), and Youth4Media Network across various countries in Europe also offer exemplars for dialogue that could lead to connected learning.

According to Soep and Chavez (2010), who describe the work of Youth Radio, media production promotes authorial and entrepreneurial practices that build on youth voices often ignored by mainstream media. They note that media production creates opportunities for broadcasting, policy impact, jobs, and higher education. Apparent in the proliferation of youth media organizations are the active roles of young people who use media production to raise key issues relevant in their lives. In the next section, I turn to remix and multimodality to frame the work of producers and artists featured in this chapter.

Remix and Multimodality in Media Production

It is worth revisiting the term *remix*. The term has been used to trace developments in music, film, literature, and other cultural forms; it has also been useful in understanding language and knowledge construction. By definition, *remix* means to appropriate, borrow, and blend texts to create new(er) texts. According to Lessig, "Whether text or beyond, remix is collage; it comes from combining elements of RO (read only) culture; it succeeds by leveraging the meaning created by the reference to build something new" (2008, 76). The technique in remix provides ease in sharing and invites a community to participate. In theorizing rhythm science, Miller, aka DJ Spooky (2004) points to music sampling as a method of advancing a musical genre. The deftness of mixing across sounds and social settings in connection to hip-hop becomes a key component of artistic production. In other words, mixing sounds is in part a manifestation of a larger remix culture that includes graffiti tagging, break dancing, DJ'ing, language, and fashion.

Today's remix practices allow for a variety of writing, including fan fiction, manga, photoshopping, and video mash-ups. An example of a video mash-up is Kutiman's "Mother of All Funk Chords," which inventively pieces together user-uploaded videos on YouTube to generate a new sound, a polyphonic global session (Yang 2012). At the heart of remix is the use of one or more modalities (oral or written language, images, symbols, sounds, gestures, artifacts, etc.) in specific semiotic domains that communicate distinctive types of meaning (Gee 2003). Remix, then, is not simply about a change in content (a derivative) but also a change in context (a different meaning). In her study of literacy and media in children's lives, Dyson suggests that children draw on their knowledge of popular cultural texts to make meaning of other texts through processes of recontextualization—that is, "differentiation, appropriation, translation, and the reframing of cultural material across symbolic forms and social practices" (2003, 108). The reframing, which in itself is a remix, produces a different meaning, and the process starts again toward the next remix. Central to that meaning are individuals' interactions with others as well as with texts; it does not preclude elements of intertextuality that link the text being designed to one or more series of existing texts (Bakhtin 1981; Fairclough 1989).

To further understand remix, it is important to draw on multimodality as a resource for meaning-making in media production (Kress 2001, 2003). Specifically, Kress and Van Leeuwen (2001) look at discourse, design, production, and distribution to understand multiple modes of communication. They note that discourse and design relate to the *content* of what is being communicated, while production and distribution relate to *expression* or the manifestation of content. In my investigation of youth media, the strata of discourse, design, production, and distribution are important because they account for what is intricately involved in the *articulation* (encoding) and *interpretation* (decoding) of text. For youth media artists, mode or the particular choice of mode becomes central in the process of production. Mode serves as a resource for representation; mode is also integral to the articulation (encoding) and interpretation (decoding) of any text, be it visual, written, or aural. Moreover, social semiotics suggests that encoding reflects the sender/writer's "grammar" while decoding captures the idiosyncrasy of audience reception (Hodge and Kress 1988). The encoding/decoding binary is without tension (Hall 1992), and the idiosyncratic uptake of texts is interpellated by discourse and ideology (Althusser 1971; Foucault 1977). In other words, any text is shaped by multiple recontextualizations and re-mediations by different creators and users in different places at different times. The locality situates any text analysis.

Using a multiperspectival lens into cultural studies, Kellner (1995) points to the interplay between articulation and interpretation to peel back layers of texts with particularized meanings. He offers a diagnostic critique using history to read texts and texts to read history. Such a dual optic allows insight into the multiple relations between texts and contexts, between media culture and history, and, as I will argue, between the social worlds of a poet/writer and a producer/filmmaker. With this in mind, I will view youths' agency and identity positions within video production (Charmaraman 2008; Halverson 2010; Hull and Katz 2006: Rogers et al. 2010) with a focus on the politics of rewriting media as a form of social critique embedded in social relations (Burwell 2010; Jocson 2010; Kellner and Kim, 2010).

Defining Critical Solidarity

As more digital remix practices develop, the link between media culture, history, and locality provides a way to understand youth producing media based on shared social critique. According to Ferguson, critical solidarity is a means by which we acknowledge the social dimensions of our thinking and analyses. It requires that we ally ourselves with others. He writes:

> Autonomy is a convenient pointer away from any easy acceptance of domination in the name of any cause. But we quickly find that our relationships to the media are not ones that can be sustained autonomously. Shared critique requires a social commitment . . . recognising the ways in which taking sides in relation to media representations has social consequences. We have to decide how we will "act" with others who share our views, and with those who do not. In this sense we have to move towards judgements and actions based upon forms of solidarity. Sometimes it may be a solidarity about which music we wish to hear or the length of our hair. At other times it may be solidarity over our understanding of justice and exploitation and our democratic rights and responsibilities. We have to recognise that, in a media age, these issues are likely to occur back to back (or screen to screen) and that they are likely to come to us first in the form of re-presentations. (2001, 42)

Noteworthy here are the interconnections between young people through their social positions on media, culture, and respect for fundamental human rights. These interconnections are arguably a form of assemblage, as noted in chapter 1. More to the point, the notion of critical solidarity draws attention to broader progressive goals of understanding and tolerance among seemingly disparate groups.

Building on Masterman's (1990) critical autonomy, critical solidarity sees individuals and groups (including youth) as having the freedom to judge for themselves the relative merits of alternative possibilities rather than being indoctrinated into a particular worldview. In this chapter, I borrow the term critical solidarity to demonstrate the relative autonomy of poets/writers and producers/filmmakers. The term is more than shared interests and social critique. As I will point out, critical solidarity is reified through a cultural and material remix as a representation of youth's social worlds. The production of a larger artistic project also exemplifies a set of creative and critical literacies to utilize written, oral/aural, and visual forms of communication as a means to challenge dominant ideologies and power relationships that underlie them (Goodman 2003; Janks 2010; Morrell 2008; Share 2009; Vasquez 2004). Critical solidarity, then, is a strategic application of creative and critical forms of literacies toward social action.

Documenting and Analyzing Media Texts

To gain some perspective, I utilized an ethnographic approach that built on existing networks from my earlier study on youth poetry in northern California. I attended and observed various community media arts events and accessed media texts online or through copies provided by the artists themselves. I was also active in following the dissemination of local youth-made films regionally and nationally. Based on my level of access to media texts and interaction with artists, I focused on two well-circulated video poem projects, "Slip of the Tongue" and "Barely Audible," in order to understand media production and distribution. Doing so provided a particular lens into how youth themselves shaped, and were being shaped by, remix culture. Data sources included semi-structured interviews with poets, artists, and producers; field notes from participant observations; collections of media or related products such as written poems (in draft or published form), audio and video recordings of spoken word performances and DVD copies of completed videos; and producer/director commentary.

I used content and multimodal analysis to make sense of the collected data; a matrix was created as an analytic tool particularly to understand the complexity of media texts (see Appendix A). The matrix took into account the technical, conceptual, and aesthetic elements of production, and the various written, visual, and aural/oral modes used to create a media text (note: the matrix doubly served as a production guide for students and teachers with whom I worked). Although the culminating media text in my study was specific to video, the table was flexible enough to be used for analyzing other modes and genres of production, such as animation and podcasts. Special attention to the technical, conceptual, and aesthetic elements of the production demonstrated the locality of uptakes and stylistic choices rendered in the video. For the purpose of this chapter, I feature "Slip of the Tongue" and "Barely Audible" to discuss the blending of script, image, and sound based on the idiosyncratic uptakes of each respective poet/writer and producer/filmmaker. Their real names are used here.[4]

"Slip of the Tongue"

The Poet/Writer

Spoken word poet Adriel Luis wrote "Slip of the Tongue." He was a freshman at a four-year public university when he first wrote the poem and yes, admittedly, "to impress a girl." He was a senior at a public high school in northern California when his interest in spoken word took shape. As a high school student he joined Youth Speaks, a literary arts organization in San Francisco, where he began to perform on stage, compete in slams, and form alliances with other spoken word artists, including a group that later became iLL-Literacy (http://ill-literacy.com). As a college student he got involved in social activism and took courses in Asian American studies and women's studies. In an interview,[5] Luis told me that before college he was a B student in Advanced Placement English, was forced to read canonical texts, and did not appreciate acts of writing (essays and poems). He critiqued the approach to studying literature as irrelevant or stereotypical:

> When the teacher tried to outreach and give an ethnic poetry
> unit, for example, it was poetry from a very token experience.
> So any time it was Asian American poetry it was something about
> food or about watching my mother scale fish. And it was like *that's
> great* but there's a lot more to the Asian American experience
> than that.

Luis also recognized the lack of books and other materials in the classroom that represented more fully different sets of Asian American experiences. While he read at home starting at an early age and listened to music as a household practice, he noted that there were rare opportunities to engage perspectives from a "young person or from an Asian American." Luis felt "that in order for there to be something, I had to create it myself." As a high school student, Luis noticed that the growing spoken word movement in the San Francisco Bay Area included Asian American artists such as 8th Wonder and I Was Born with Two Tongues, with whom he was becoming familiar through local events. The connection to other Asian Americans was a salient juncture shaping his sense of critical solidarity. He noted:

When you're part of a movement, it really helps you feel the passion because then you realize that not only are you producing this
for yourself but there are actually people out there that are feeling
it and looking for it too. For everybody who was like me as a high-
schooler looking for that, not even fathoming that it existed in the
first place, there was this time of discovery. And so it was these
spoken word artists that jumpstarted it . . . and I would stay up
late my freshman year [in college] researching all this stuff and
taking courses . . . as a male growing up, it was kind of an awak-
ening. I was really blind to all this stuff so I wanted to write about
something I had always kind of felt inside.

In light of his shifting views and identity position, Luis was intrigued
by the concept of makeup and "flipped it" to pursue a poem from the
perspective of an Asian American woman. He recounted the writing
process that led to an early printed version of "Slip of the Tongue,"
which first appeared in a university campus paper. Then a recorded
version of the poem was included in a CD album entitled *Bringing the
Noise* released by Youth Speaks. Not long after that, in 2006, "Slip of
the Tongue" was published as part of Luis' first chapbook, *How To Make
Juice.* These printed and recorded versions, according to Luis, are different from the actual poem narration in the video "Slip of the Tongue."
The changes in the poem suggest a recurring practice of revision with
purpose, format, and audience in mind. Luis noted that he eventually
put the poem to rest but was urged by others to revisit it again. He
shared the following:

My poems are always constantly changing. It's not like I sit down
and do one revision and then like four months later another
one. The first version was like eight minutes long because I went
through every single kind of makeup like finger nail polish, blush,
and all this stuff. . . . I did it at one open mic and realized it was
rather long . . . the "Slip of the Tongue" version that I did at the
slam was the first official version, cut down from eight minutes
to four. That's the one the film uses. In 2005, I wasn't performing
the poem anymore because I felt like my writing had advanced
and I was writing about other things. But when the poem started

getting more attention, through the film, I kind of felt like I wanted to perform it again because people were coming up to me and requesting the poem.

Luis performed "Slip of the Tongue" and the performance was recorded. The use of intonation and voice inflection, for example, suggests the interplay of multiple senses, or transduction, in his work. As Luis pointed out, the poem narration in the video "Slip of the Tongue" was cut down to four minutes and streamlined in order to appeal to a broader audience. The recorded poem begins with:

My glares burn through her
And I'm sure that such actions aren't foreign to her
because the essence of her beauty is, well, the essence of beauty . . .[6]

The Producer/Filmmaker

From the performed and recorded poem came the video "Slip of the Tongue" produced by Karen Lum. She was in the ninth grade attending a public high school in northern California when she first witnessed one of Adriel's performances of "Slip of the Tongue" at a local slam event. Soon after, she realized the poem's potential for a multimedia Public Service Announcement (PSA) project. Karen was an active member of an after-school program called Youth Sounds/The Factory (now merged with the Bay Area Video Coalition, or BAVC), a place where young people can access media technologies and gain various media production skills. The following is an excerpt from Karen's explanation of the project's beginnings:

Slip of the Tongue originated when I was asked to participate in a filmmakers conference in Connecticut in 2005. In order to go, I had to produce a one-minute PSA that incorporated the theme of how youth are making a difference. Being a lover of spoken word, I wrote out a vague treatment about how many youth utilize poetry to change the world through self-expression. The organizers of the conference immediately rejected my treatment and told me that I needed to have a solid story line. Then one day, the idea suddenly came to me. I would take a poetry recording and apply images to it. The slam poem Slip of the Tongue by my friend stood out to me since it actually told a story and was structured just like a film with an introduction, conflict, climax and resolution. And so after 2 weeks, I finished my 1 minute PSA, and eventually, it turned into a complete 4 minute short. (Media That Matters Film Festival 2007)

The video "Slip of the Tongue" (total running time 4:06) is based on Adriel's live performance of the poem. The tagline "girl meets boy at a bus stop" captures the opening scene of a rather complex stance on ethnicity, gender, and media culture. By 2008, the video had been screened in over fifty film festivals and garnered twelve awards, including the Northern California Emmy Award for Best Youth Film and the Jury Award from Media That Matters Film Festival. The video also became available for streaming online through UthTV, ListenUp!, Independent Movie Database (IMDb), and YouTube. Many of these outlets no longer carry it, although the video remains on YouTube. In 2014, Karen re-uploaded "Slip of the Tongue" as part of a new line of work involving media production called Womanly State of Mind which began taking shape during her time as a student at Stanford University.[7]

The success of "Slip of the Tongue" suggests the untapped potential in youth media. The video's *content* (discourse and design) and *expression* (production and distribution) partly shaped the artists' ability to reach a larger audience. However, the modes embedded in the making of "Slip of the Tongue" are worth exploring. First, there is the level of the script, the poem written by Adriel. Second, there is the level of image, shot, sequenced, and repurposed by Karen. Third, there is the level of sound, the majority of which is provided by Adriel's voice and the audience reaction from the live performance. Street noise and other background sounds were included during editing.

Of interest here is remix—the appropriation and (re)assembling of an already existing text (the original poem) and the ways in which the written/performed poem was (re)designed using particular tools to create a video poem. According to Karen, the editing software program Final Cut Pro was key in composing this remixed multimodal text. Just as important in the production process were the various preproduction steps that shaped the making of the video. These steps included scouting locations, acquiring permission to shoot, identifying actors, putting together a production crew, storyboarding, rehearsing, configuring lighting, and coordinating the best times to shoot given the logic in the narrative. DIY and DIT production proved to be significant for Karen. She noted:

> I basically made the film by myself. I shot a lot of those scenes whenever I could do it myself. I had a tripod, so I just set it up and hit record and ran in front of the camera and did something and then ran back and hit record again. I had some help though. Some of my friends at Youth Sounds, they helped me with some shots I couldn't do by myself, but I did the editing. I did the editing myself. It was a one-person crew because initially I didn't expect anyone to see the film so I treated it like a small little project, and then it blew up.

For Karen, it was important to draw on Youth Sounds for material and human resources to complete her video project. At the conclusion of the video, Karen credited Youth Sounds, her older brother (a filmmaker), and Will Tsang (a filmmaker and an actor in the video). She also acknowledged Adriel, whose words drove the essence behind the video:

> The whole film was narrated by the poem so my idea was to convert it into a film. All I did was put images on top of his words. I didn't change anything, and I just filmed stuff that was relevant to the words of the poem, and then I made the film.

Evident in the video are similarities and differences in Adriel's and Karen's experiences that merged into one text. A comparative analysis of both texts yields insights into each creator's use of pastiche, parody, irony, and hyperbole. For the purposes of this discussion, it is important to highlight the references to gender, ethnicity, body, and place to suggest the locality of uptakes. Karen described at length how the poem resonated with her:

> My mentor at Youth Sounds always tells me to put a little bit of myself into my films, well, in this one, I put myself entirely in it. But, the premise is a moment. I used to take the bus all the time, like what goes on in the poem. So when I listened to the poem,

I imagined it at a bus stop because that's totally me. That's what I do, that's very Oakland taking the AC transit, and I wanted to include that aspect of my life and my culture into the film. So, I just brainstormed. Adriel is talking about makeup or reading through magazines and stuff, and the thing is the poem really affected me because I totally related to it. I grew up in a majority white area. There's nothing wrong with that, but I grew up entirely around people who were not my color. And so, growing up, all my friends were white. I thought being white was beautiful. Listening to the poem kind of affected how I feel about my beauty and my self-esteem. So, I just included things [in the film] that felt natural to me, like looking through magazines, seeing white models as pretty, brunette as pretty, but never seeing Asian girls, and to me that was my standard of beauty. Things weren't attainable through these standards. Over time, I overcame that and now I'm proud of who I am. That's how "Slip of the Tongue" really affected me and that's why I chose the poem, to reach a lot of people.

Karen's adaptation of Adriel's poem reflects a process of becoming, a way of understanding self and constructing identity through media production (Charmaraman 2008). The video "Slip of the Tongue" repurposed through editing pays tribute to Adriel's performance and signifies Karen's social worlds. Critical solidarity between the poet/writer and producer/filmmaker resulted in a film that is also a product of identity (Asian American) and a product of social critique (gender, ethnicity, body, and place).

"Barely Audible"

The Poet-Writer

Chinaka Hodge is a spoken word artist, writer, educator, and playwright from Oakland, California.[8] Her acclaimed work has been featured in various nationally recognized magazines and newspapers and on national radio and television shows, including HBO's Def Poetry. Her first independently written play, *Mirrors in Every Corner,* was commissioned by San Francisco's Intersection for the Arts and opened in the spring of 2010. Chinaka was one of twelve selected writers from around the world to participate in the 2013 Sundance Screenwriters Lab. She is a graduate of New York University's Gallatin School of the Arts and University of Southern California's School of Cinematic Arts (Writing for Screen and Television); currently, she is an associate director for programs and pedagogy at Yerba Buena Center in San Francisco while continuing to write and perform in various capacities.

Chinaka began to write at an early age. Her father gave her a journal for every birthday and insisted on journal writing as a daily activity. She wrote her first poem at four years old. Then some years later, a teacher in the midst of a public school strike asked her and other students to conduct a research project on the history of African Americans. She recalled the following:

> I think my biggest formative year was in the sixth grade. I had to write a two-page report. For a sixth grader, it was okay. I ended up writing my report and was really fascinated by the fact that all the foul stuff happened to black folks that I never heard about even through my very militant family. And then the power that the work had for me and others to kind of bring it to light. I finished it and felt like I was participating in history, something that was important to me.
>
> Then, I also participated in an essay-writing competition, around the time the Cypress Freeway fell down [during the Loma Prieta earthquake in 1989]. They rebuilt the structure, and there was an unveiling where poems and essays written by West Oakland youth about the future of transportation were featured. My essay won the prize for best essay. And so, that was kind of like seeing that I could write and that there was some tangible reward—I could make a living. I won a computer.

In the ninth grade, Chinaka took an interest in Youth Speaks when a program representative conducted a writing workshop in her English class. Chinaka recalled her subsequent involvement in activities both inside and outside school to further develop as a writer. In an interview, she noted her literary influences who included both seasoned and novice writers, some of whom were her mentors and peers at Youth Speaks. Chinaka competed in poetry slams for several years and earned the title grand slam youth poet as a junior in high school. That year, during a national poetry slam, she wrote "Barely Audible." She revealed the following about her writing process:

I wrote that [poem] about fifteen minutes before leaving the house for the final slam. I had this other poem that I was doing. A poem about my mom or something like that. But it was the first time I had ever written anything that long. Most of my first ones were shorter, and I ended up winning with it. I was basically attaching a sound to a feeling, a sound to an experience, a neighborhood. And so I did that, and it was the first [time] I used sound to convey a point. I remember kind of like piecing it together and not getting to finish it until really right before we walked out the door and being really like, "This is gonna suck but I'm gonna do it anyway." And people back then were like, "What are you gonna do? Don't you have it memorized?" And I was like, "Yeah, I got paper. We'll see what happens." I have grown tremendously as a writer since then. I wrote it when I was seventeen, and so much in my life has changed. I'm a tremendously different person now. But all the issues [in the poem] are still really important and resonate with a lot of people.

Similar to Adriel's writing process, the original "Barely Audible" poem from that slam competition has since been revised at different times for different purposes. The following opening lines are represented in the video:

it's 3:30
I'm watching potential martyrs from my window
got my nose pressed against the glass
the sidewalk is drab, grey, dull, cracked . . .[9]

The Filmmaker-Producer

Eli Jacobs-Fantauzzi is an independent filmmaker who is partly responsible for the video "Barely Audible." Eli studied at New York University's Tisch School of the Arts and first met Chinaka when she was a junior in high school in the San Francisco Bay Area. Their connection as artists grew with a shared love for hip-hop, crossing paths at open mics, hip-hop in the park jams, and artist retreats. During his first semester of graduate school at Tisch, Eli and his classmates were tasked with an assignment to create a short video. He recalled:

> I decided to go beyond what was asked of us [my project team Vivian Wenli Li and Kathleen Copeland] . . . to make a video that could showcase our skills and have a strong social message. Immediately, I remembered Chinaka's poem "Barely Audible," which she had just performed at the Bowery Poetry Club [in New York City]. While listening to the poem, I was already mentally creating how this could be represented cinematically. I asked the members of the group if they would be interested in creating a visual interpretation of her poem. We all agreed and had Chinaka come record the poem in the school's recording booth.

Of interest to Eli and his fellow project members as film students was the cinematic possibility within the poem. The poem went through a process of recontextualization, a kind of remix attending to differentiation, appropriation, translation, and the reframing of existing cultural material. He shared the following:

> The next step [for us] was sitting down and creating a storyboard. We listened to the poem over and over, and wrote down the images that came to mind. Our goal was to not simply show what Chinaka described in her poem. We wanted to create parallel stories connected to larger issues. We decided to use imagery and sounds that would help place the viewers in the lives of the characters as well as feel some of their anxiety and desperation. Chinaka places herself in the poem, watching the kids down below from her window. So we decided to use that as the opening shot, starting more literally and getting more abstract as the poem goes on. At first, we saw it as a dilemma that we were in Brooklyn and not in Oakland, California, where the story in the original poem takes place. After some time, we agreed that the issues of poverty, gentrification, and violence were affecting youth all over the country and we could show that these problems were bigger than Oakland.

With DIY and DIT production, Eli and his team shot the video by putting together a community of artists and friends. Various local individuals in New York were recruited to take part and appear in the video. Eli identified who was involved to cinematically re-create and repurpose "Barely Audible":

> We recruited Nyoka Acevedo, an educator and activist, to take the lead role as Trina. Divine, aka Don Divino, who worked closely with Dead Prez, played the role of Darius. We counted on our friends, our students, and their parents to all come and play different roles for our video.

Upon completion of the video, Eli and his team went on to share it with as many people as possible. The video was screened in film festivals, universities, classrooms, and after-school programs; as well, it was broadcast nationally on PBS. As the video gained recognition through multiple screenings, Chinaka also continued to perform the poem at poetry slams and other events, including HBO's Def Poetry.

Since their initial collaboration, Eli and Chinaka as artists have become great friends and have worked together on other projects. The latest collaboration is Life Is Living, an arts festival centered on sustainability in urban communities (Joseph and Cook, 2013). Eli serves as a videographer.[10] In recounting the process of recontextualization of "Barely Audible," Eli revealed key connections between the poem, the video, and the festival:

> [Chinaka] wrote the poem "Barely Audible" on 18th Street and Myrtle, just a few blocks from Lil' Bobby Hutton Park [also known as DeFremery Park] where we decided to have the Life Is Living festival. As a community effort, the festival was created to address many of the issues presented in the poem. Our methods, our projects, and our visions as artists may have changed but our commitment to justice stays constant. When we meet other literary and media artists around the country—whether they are students, teachers, or peers—with the same mission, we form an alliance, and that is how we have created this movement. It is important to us to ally with others, blending our artistic work, whatever it may be, with community work.

Locality of Uptakes: A Closer Look at the Videos

Both "Slip of the Tongue" and "Barely Audible" signal stylistic choices in multimedia composition and the role of remix in youth media. Multimodal analysis suggests the locality of idiosyncratic uptakes by producers/filmmakers. For "Slip of the Tongue," locations included Oakland's Chinatown and downtown area (store sidewalks, street signs, a bus stop, a cafe, and a restaurant); Karen's house (bedroom, bathroom, living room, kitchen with a breakfast table, patio-balcony); Karen's family owned video store (aisles and shelves); and the Youth Sounds building (elevator and hallway). Wide-angle shots were common to capture the physical environment. To emphasize particular signs, Karen used close-ups of street names, images of women in magazines and other media, body curves, family portraits, and a Confucian quote. The articulation of localized meanings set the overall tone and shaped the logic of the video. Karen's "Slip of the Tongue" took on a narrative of its own, building upon Adriel's take on makeup, and (re)assembling it to convey a particular stance about standards of beauty through a particular Asian American experience. Depictions of a young woman brought up in a Chinese American family reveal complex negotiations with American society, negotiations primed by race, ethnicity, gender, culture, body, and place. The discourse widens from "girl meets boy at a bus stop" to a nuanced response to the question, "What is your ethnic makeup?"

In addition to particularized meanings, Karen in a director's commentary pointed out the significance of cinematic influences in the video. Key figures such as Hong Kong filmmaker Wong Kar-Wai were prominent in her rendition of "Slip of the Tongue." Wong is known for his film-noir style and use of vivid imagery. Upon a closer examination of "Slip of the Tongue," I found that Karen accentuated various scenes by adjusting granularity, contrasts, and hues to add a lush color palette with Wong's filmmaking style in mind. For example, the colors blue, yellow, green, and red are traceable as a purposeful aesthetic effect. Karen's interpretation of Wong's style had been (re)articulated in her design and production. In further examining Wong's films *In the Mood for Love* (2000) and *Happy Together* (1997), Karen's stylistic choices—borrowed and appropriated—blurred the line between amateur and professional videography. The affordance of remix and multimodality with access to camera, lighting, and production equipment allowed for "Slip of the

Tongue" to be created in such high quality. Since its release, the video has reached various audiences across the globe via film festivals and social media.

For "Barely Audible," it is evident how the social worlds detailed in Chinaka's poem transcend one location and are recontextualized in another. Eli and his team used visual modes to augment meanings embedded in the poem. This is important because it demonstrates a process of meaning-making (decoding) that helped to shape the creation (encoding) of another text. Come to think of it, isn't that what we ask of our students in the classroom through reading and writing instruction? Isn't that what we ask of young people participating in literary or media arts programs and other youth-based organizations? The intertextual nature of "Barely Audible" from the written poem to the video poem is apparent.

Locations in "Barely Audible" included sidewalks, street signs, buildings, and a liquor store in Brooklyn, New York. Similar to Karen's stylistic choices, wide-angle shots were common to capture the physical environment. To emphasize particular signs, Eli and his team used close-ups of street names as well as actors' bodies and faces. The articulation of localized meanings set the overall tone and shaped the logic of the video. "Barely Audible" took on a different yet similar narrative, assembling and reassembling particularized meanings conveyed in the original poem. Depictions of Darius and Trina in the context of Oakland (in the poem) and Brooklyn (in the video) revealed the connections between two communities. The discourse widens from the local in Oakland— "18th and Myrtle"—to the translocal in Brooklyn—"it's time to care." Both versions conveyed social issues such as poverty, gentrification, and violence, with subtle and explicit references to race, ethnicity, gender, history, time, and place. The locality of uptakes in the video marked a combined social critique.

In addition to particularized meanings, Eli pointed out in a director's commentary the significance of cinematic influences in the video. Key figures such as New York–based filmmaker Spike Lee were prominent in choosing camera angles and composition. Lee is known for his use of dolly-tracking shots and filming in the streets of Brooklyn. Such stylistic choices are traceable in "Barely Audible." Eli's interpretation of Lee's style had been rearticulated in the design and production of the video. With its multimodal composition and opportunities for cultural and material remix, "Barely Audible" exemplifies how the work of young people can be further legitimized in digital media culture. The active distribution of youth-made films through film festivals and social media expands the possibilities of (re)articulation and (re)interpretation in different contexts. Only time will tell how critical solidarity will again take shape between poets/writers and producers/filmmakers as they continue to blur the lines between amateurism and professionalism. What new and existing works will propel young people to use media production and remix as a form of social critique and social action? What material and pedagogical resources will be available to them? In what ways can educators and other adult allies support young people in their pursuit of critical solidarity?

Intersections of Literary and Media Arts

There is untapped potential in the intersections of literary and media arts. "Slip of the Tongue" and "Barely Audible" are noteworthy in their own right, and I offer them here to underscore the future of youth media. These works are indicative of a DIY to DIT approach to media production that provides the poet/writer and the producer/filmmaker an opportunity to appropriate, tinker, and repurpose meaning (de Certeau 1984). The videos' content (discourse and design) and expression (production and distribution) shaped the artists' ability to reach a large audience. In practical terms, the videos are now being used in writing, video production, and related workshops where discussions about remix, collaboration, and the power of storytelling create opportunities for envisioning other artistic and cultural projects toward social transformation.

However, pedagogical possibilities go beyond what the poet/writer and producer/filmmaker did; rather, the recontextualization of cultural material supposes alternative practices for blending genres as a form of cultural politics—wherever the creator or producer might be in a particular space and time. Central to the production process was remix— the appropriation, assembling, and reassembling of an already existing text (the original poem) and how the written and performed poem was designed and redesigned with particular tools to create a video or visual poem. The remix illuminates similarities and differences in the artists' experiences as individuals committed to social transformation— similarities and differences that merged into one text.

As I have increasingly observed in high school classrooms, the (re)mixing of poetry as one form of media production can open up doors for understanding literature and for expanding writing instruction (Applebee and Langer 2013). What we know is that young people are adapting existing texts, whether the material is produced by peers or extracted from textbooks and supplementary sources. Young people are also finding creative ways to appropriate, design, and produce other texts, whether on their own or with others. The concept of remix is certainly not new. With today's media technologies, remix invigorates what is happening and what is possible in content area classrooms and other educational settings. If interpretation (reading) and articulation (writing/producing)—through the strata of design, discourse, production, and distribution—are key in the multimodal process (Kress and Van Leeuwen 2001), then how might media production in social studies or English/language arts classrooms be further conceived?

Recall Ms. Gantry and Ms. Byrd in chapter 1. To complement Ms. Gantry's effort to incorporate digital media technology into her social studies curriculum, English teacher Ms. Byrd assigned William Shakespeare's *Romeo and Juliet* to students. The reading of the book led to the creation of a multimedia project (video) that prompted students to write and design a screenplay, go on location at different parts of the school and the surrounding community, enact a number of scenes, and shoot video footage with local actors (students in the class). Specifically, the story of the Capulets and the Montagues was interpreted and (re)articulated in a way that enabled students to demonstrate their understanding and recontextualize the rivalry between two families in the present day. Along with the rivalry, the overarching love story was appropriated in a student-produced song laced with a student-produced beat that later became a featured track in a thirty-minute video called *Romeo and Juliet, Part Deux*. The opportunity for material and cultural remix was a polysemic exercise for students to play out various possible meanings. Remix and multimodality offered students idiosyncratic uptakes of the text which culminated in a set of multimedia compositions.

Separately and collectively, "Slip of the Tongue" and "Barely Audible" allow us to see the potential of youth media at the intersection of literary and media arts. Both examples teach us to envision pedagogical possibilities that would further enable human capacities through media production. That is, we might just learn something crucial from youth themselves about how to render education differently. The DIY and DIT approach to media production as present in the work of poets/writers and producers/filmmakers is tied to teaching and learning. First, media production reaffirms the varied levels of interests and participation of young people in the growing movement in literary and media arts. Second, media production suggests the need to expand our perspectives on what young people have to say and how they engage in making media within participatory cultures. Third, media production pushes us to rethink the teaching/learning paradigm, at the very least questioning who is an expert or who is a novice.

Often in classrooms, teachers take on a role as authoritative figures and sole knowledge producers, and students are treated as passive receptors and consumers. What if teachers became learners, and students became more active facilitators of learning? What might classrooms look or sound like with new conversations and altered interactions between teachers and students? It is a hopeful endeavor as many young people are at the forefront of experimenting with innovations in media technology. Finally, media production reinforces the importance of arts education through the building of strong ties between students, teachers, community members, and artists as partners in education. Literary and media arts can offer a place from which to draw a range of ideas relevant to literacy, teaching, and learning.

Remix in education and the notion of youth media as critical solidarity challenges educators to consider the different ways young people are:

- building on each other's talents, skills, and experiences;
- working together as critical consumers and producers to create new(er) multimodal texts;
- disrupting dominant notions regarding the way things should be;
- pushing the field of youth media and blurring the lines between amateurs and professionals;
- distributing high-quality multimedia products to reach larger audiences in shaping media culture, history, and society.

The opportunity for material and cultural remix is upon us. As we have seen, the use of different modes with young people coming together in the production process has implications for education. How might high schools support projects where content area classes work together with literary and media arts organizations? What might a collaboration between high school and college students look like? What might a translation of traditional texts into multimodal texts or other artistic forms offer? What cultural meanings and representations might surface in media production (script, image, sound) that otherwise would not surface in print alone? What might it mean to practice encoding (articulation) and decoding (interpretation) in ways that explicitly connect the social realities of young people locally, regionally, and globally? With more and more young people forming social alliances, in what ways might emerging practices lead to larger artistic projects toward social transformation? We might not have all the answers. But there are exemplars at the intersection of literary and media arts that point us in the right direction.

What Now?

To this day, the poems and videos discussed in this chapter find their way into my university courses. It is incredibly humbling to have known the poets/writers and producers/filmmakers when they were first just starting out and making a name for themselves. They are now well into their adulthood and are pursuing various artistic and professional pathways. Their acclaimed works have endured the test of time. I must say, the poems and the videos continue to be instructive. What holds true is the idea that young people are coming together with shared interests and social critique. They are using digital media technology across genre practices (spoken word poetry and filmmaking). They are creating media and recognizing their social consequences. Put simply, youth media as critical solidarity at the very least means sharing information that takes into account humanistic, social, historical, political, and economic contexts. It means embracing the interrelationships and consequences of everyday actions, experiences, and lifestyles (Ferguson 2001). It means being independent and interdependent critical thinkers, and forming social alliances across contexts, genres, and media platforms.

For educators, it is important to develop a range of innovative approaches to build on critical solidarity to address present-day challenges in education. We are seeing more and more teachers and students engaged in youth media work.[11] Recent initiatives and programs such as World Savvy in San Francisco, Youth Media Collaborative in

Philadelphia, and YOUmedia in Chicago have provided spaces for young people to inspire new works. The Kennedy Center in Washington, D.C., began a national campaign called "What's Going On Now?" as a way to highlight youth-produced media and to raise awareness about social issues relevant to young people across several U.S. cities. The campaign draws on Marvin Gaye's 1971 song "What's Going On" as a point of departure for a cultural and material remix using a multimedia platform of video, music, and social commentary. The campaign coincides with new directions in digital media and connected learning where young people, their interests, and their talents are at the center of the dialogue. The next chapter discusses the work of more youth who produced a television broadcast in a multimedia communications classroom. The focus shifts to youth media as place-making.

3

Place-Making in Career and Technical Education

The sun was beaming through cirrus clouds. It was eighty degrees in St. Louis, Missouri. It had rained the night before, keeping the humidity level low. The eight fountains in the Grand Basin spouted synchronously. I was on Art Hill in Forest Park contemplating a conversation I had had with a teacher about students and person–environment relations in education. The conversation, which took place inside the history museum, aimed to generate ideas about school–community connections. There, in that moment of respite sitting on a patch of grass, I noticed the sky's image reflecting in the water a few yards away, with the museum edifice visible in the background. People in paddleboats were moving at their own pace, flowing freely, changing directions here and there—some reaching into the water and splashing themselves. To me, this was a figurative reminder of what happens in educational settings, where students interact with the environment in multiple ways, and vice versa. I panned my surroundings and trekked to the bottom of the hill, where an arched bridge serves as an overpass above the boat paddlers. Weeks later, I would return to that same spot after meeting with a high school teacher interested in doing a multimedia project that centered on the local environment. I realized then that that particular meeting in the museum was key to our thinking about place and learning ecologies.

This chapter builds on previous chapters to illuminate how place is integral to youth media production. I draw on an ethnographic study in the context of high school multimedia communications within Career and Technical Education (CTE). Place-based approaches were central to students' collaborative inquiry projects, which culminated in a television broadcast that students aptly named "Put Us on the Map." A CTE teacher and I built on conjectures to create and extend learning opportunities. To account for the influence of person–environment relations in human learning (Barron 2006; Bronfenbrenner 1994), a learning ecology was engineered to include the classroom, the classroom's television studio, a community resource center, and the school district's television station. The study illustrates place as relational and contingent upon relationships as students move within and across the learning ecology. To prepare for the television broadcast, students conducted research on educational and social issues such as high school graduation rates, poverty and unemployment, gang violence, and teen pregnancy. This collaborative inquiry process included online search, use of geospatial mapping, and completion of analytic writing that took the form of a public service announcement (PSA), slideshow, and op-ed video. Using various media production tools such as iPhoto, iMovie, Videocue, and Wirecast, students created prerecorded segments to be incorporated into a live broadcast on the school's television network. In analyzing Put Us on the Map in segments and as a whole, students constructed relational experiences as racialized, gendered, and minoritized youth in order to enter, alter, and disrupt dominant discourses of educational and social issues affecting their lives. In large part, what students produced was shaped by neoliberal reforms in redefining public education, except here it was students' tacit knowledge at the center of discourse.

Media production was an opportunity to push back against stringent conceptions of learning, to position students not as passive consumers but as active producers of knowledge, and to reframe educational goals with youth and community voices at the fore. What I present in this chapter points to the value of place-based media production in CTE for developing students' literate repertoires and weaving students' lives into their learning in the service of place-making. Before moving to that discussion, let me turn to relevant literature in conceptualizing place to understand place-based media production.

Place-Based Approaches and Literacy Studies

In the past decade, place-based approaches have increasingly gained attention in the field of education and shaped teaching and learning practices in support of students across social contexts. The notion of place as lived space with dynamic networks, shaped by and constituting cultures and identities, has been influential in pushing investigations that emphasize people's relationship to their environments and habitats. Specifically, in the area of literacy studies, researchers and practitioners have borrowed from place-based education (PBE) to innovate literacy curriculum and pedagogy in expanding mandated curriculum (Comber

2011; Comber, Nixon, and Reid 2007), content area instruction (Lesley and Matthews 2009), and composition through digital storytelling (Chisholm and Trent 2014). More than this, researchers and practitioners have been attentive to changing local environments where critical literacy becomes central to inquiry projects conducted by students to examine community and school gardens, neighborhoods undergoing changes, and school designs, among others (Comber et al. 2006; Comber and Nixon 2013; also see Azano 2011). The idea that schools are meeting places (Comber 2013) provides a lens for how students negotiate contingent relationships while also developing their literate repertoires or range of cultural and linguistic practices.[1]

While PBE may be implicit in their analysis, literacy scholars in their studies of youth literacy practices in a variety of settings have demonstrated ways in which place can be useful for increasing student engagement in school, promoting literacy and academic development, and connecting learning to individual and social transformation, particularly among racialized, gendered, and minoritized youth (see Kinloch 2009; Morrell 2008; Vasudevan and DeJaynes 2013; Winn 2011). In my own research, I have broadened views of literacy by building on ecological and geospatial perspectives to examine literacy as fluid in youth's lives (Jocson 2016a; Jocson and Thorne-Wallington, 2013). I have also worked with educators, youth advocates, artists, and scholars to think more comprehensively about education in exploring the link between literacy, culture, and pedagogies of possibility across geographic lines (Jocson 2013). With continued advances in technology, I am concerned with the shifting ontological and practical dimensions of literacy in relation to place. By ontological, I mean the nature of one's being or becoming that is in constant shift. By practical, I mean one's actual doing or enacting as situated in particular contexts. My current interests in literacy and digital media have forced me to think more capaciously about place and how some youth signal place-making through youth media production. Let me now turn to the literature on place.

Place in Theory

In engaging place in research, Tuck and McKenzie (2015) outline some considerations for what they call critical place inquiry. They conceptualize place by drawing on the developments of postmodern, spatial, new materialist, and other "turns" in social research; as well, they foreground the importance of land and contributions of Indigenous epistemologies to offer insights into theory, methodology, and methods of place. Central to their scholarship is the careful treatment of place, a concept that is not easily defined given its relation to space and the various philosophical traditions (and revivals) of place. I acknowledge their push to deepen our understandings of place. For the purposes of place-based media production in this chapter, I borrowed from Lefebvre (1991) and Soja (1989, 2010) in earlier studies I conducted to understand place as lived space, not as fixed but rather as shaped by values and meanings. Place may be specific and localized but also remains grounded and connected to other places (Agnew 2011; Casey 2009).[2] As illustrated by students in their work, place is shaped by a constellation of networks and builds on the notion of place as relational, moving, and changing over time (Massey 2005).

Such consideration is attentive to new media technologies connecting people across distance, migrations of people, and circulations of information that have been deemed the spheres of life (see Appadurai 1996). Yet to say that everyone is connected because of local–global flows simplifies the complexity of place. It should be acknowledged that local places are as much a part of constructing the global as the global is constituted by different places (near or far). That is to say, an understanding of place as open, as a particular constellation within the wider contours of space, is key to understanding boundary crossings (Massey 2005).[3] Place has shifting dynamics and trajectories that pose questions about mobility, negotiation, and "throwntogetherness" (i.e., coming together at a specific time-space) without assuming natural belongingness to a place. As a product of social relations, place can also be conceived as a "meeting place" or an "intersection" imbued with social meanings, power relations, and the politics of place. This means that there are overlapping, sometimes conflicting, social realities that must be negotiated. Thinking of place as practiced can be helpful because place may be contested and (re)imagined in practical ways (Creswell 2004).

Place within Education

In education, the multidisciplinary construct of place has been vital to extend pedagogical practices. Emphasizing place in place-based or place-conscious education can arguably make teaching and learning "more relevant to the lived experience of students and teachers" so that places matter in tangible ways (Gruenewald 2003a, 260).[4] Seeing place as a source of learning becomes all the more important in an era of accountability and standardization. With increased interest in place-based approaches in education, the conceptualization of place as local or bounded to a particular community or isolated from what happens in school requires careful attention. According to Nespor, it is important to "distinguish among different historical, geographical, cultural, political, economic, and other dimensions of place construction" and to steer clear of an "idealized image of 'place' as a stable, bounded, self-sufficient communal realm" (2008, 478–9). Such consideration attends to issues of difference among varied social groups and the complexities of place and place-making. The challenge remains, however, for educators who seek to understand the possibilities of place, how place is constituted, and how places are connected to one another.

The notion of place as relational through the creation of translocal networks (or the connections beyond the local) is vital for understanding how education and schooling practices are organized. The circuits of exchange between human and more-than-human worlds, including new forms of technology, can also be generative for understanding how the material is mutually producing or enacting. One's location cannot be reduced to geometrical considerations of place (Barad 2007). That is, there are topological questions about boundary and connectivity that inform one's ways of being and becoming in the world. Put simply, a new materialist approach to place in education foregrounds the dynamics of space, time, *and* matter. Understanding that matter is enlivened and enlivening is helpful for understanding the material ontologies of place and place-making. Thus, in expanding ideas about youth media I bring together conceptualizations of place that have evolved from the work of interdisciplinary scholars in order to theorize and analyze place-based media production. This chapter underscores notions of place as relational by illuminating how students negotiated movement within and across a learning ecology in the service of place-making. What follows demonstrates the explicit treatment of place in a study situated within high school multimedia communications as a domain of learning.

Note on the Research

Briefly, I describe some of the intricacies of an educational partnership aimed at expanding learning opportunities to innovate curriculum and instruction in serving low-income minoritized youth interested in the arts and technology in the urban Midwest. Notions of place as relational and contingent, shaped by and constituting identities and cultures, triggered initial conversations between a high school multimedia communications teacher and a university literacy researcher (the author) to create learning opportunities that had direct bearing on youth's everyday lives. It was important to consider place as tied to eco-cultural resources and ecologies of learning (Barron 2006; Gutiérrez and Arzubiaga 2012; Lee 2010). Two research questions guided the study: (1) how can notions of place as relational shape learning opportunities for students in and out of the classroom, and (2) in what ways can place-based media production engage students' interests in the arts and technology?

To answer these questions, I took on a dual role as a researcher and collaborator in the multimedia communications classroom (Fine 1994). This role gradually grew to include navigating other school settings and community partner sites. Methodologically, the qualitative nature of the inquiry necessitated building rapport with school members in order to be part of an interpretive community; my entry into the high school, and eventually the classroom, was prompted by initial school site visits and conversations with an African American male CTE teacher, Mr. Miles (pseudonym), about the possibility of creating learning opportunities through school–community connections. Mr. Miles and I were key in the research design; both of us believed that a partnership could incite exciting ways of linking learning, literacy, and technology in the multimedia communications classroom. This was important as a pedagogical response to neoliberal reforms in education redefining learning goals in the context of CTE.

A one-year ethnographic study easily turned into two years in the field. Important to note is how the study's design coincided with conjectures in space-time. From the start, Mr. Miles and I were attentive to students' reason(s) for enrolling in multimedia communications, their level of engagement with media technology, and their academic and social interests inside and outside of school. We believed that understanding students' interests would help us think through possible ways of extending learning opportunities beyond the classroom.

The Put Us on the Map project was produced during a portion of our 2010–2012 work in the field. The following is an overview of the production process:

Locations:

- School, Classroom, Studio (September 2010–April 2012)
- Community Center (September 2010–November 2010)
- School District TV Station (November–December 2010)

1. Pre-Production (September–October)

- Review of media technology **in the classroom**
- Introduction to advanced tools and software (media production, mapping)
- Mapping routes assignment
- Watch and analyze clips of local news broadcasts
- Watch and analyze youth-produced media
- Introduction to op-ed genre
- Initial conversation about topics for inquiry-based op-ed projects
- Showcase of mapping routes and dialogue at **community center**

2. In-Production (October–November)

- Selection of op-ed topics **in the classroom**
- Brainstorm topics and modes of inquiry
- Gather information (personal experience, interview, online search) **in the classroom and school**
- Writing Process: drafting, editing, scripting
- Practice reading script using teleprompter
- Introduction to industry equipment and record segment at **school district television station**
- Select slideshow images and sound **in the classroom**
- Create slideshow

3. Post-Production (November–December)

- Transfer of files from student computers to main computer **in the classroom**
- Edit slideshow and recorded segments for broadcast
- Live broadcast of intro and outro "Put Us on the Map Part I"; playback of slideshows and recorded segments **in the classroom television studio**

Part I was broadcast in December 2010 at a total running time (TRT) of 20:07 minutes. Segments were as follows:

1. **Intro: Broadcast live (TRT 5:15)**
   - Pam and David: Intro

2. **Recorded segments/scripts, slideshows (TRT 13:40)**
   - Celso: "Gang Violence"
   - Han: "Drugs"
   - Carla: "Poverty and Unemployment"
   - Pam: "Teen Pregnancy"
   - David and Lamar: "High School Graduation Rates"

3. **Outro: Broadcast live (TRT 1:12)**

Building on design experiments in education (Cobb et al. 2003), the pragmatic and theoretical orientation of design-based research (iterative, interventionist, and generative) allowed for engineering and studying forms of learning that were not only consistent with possible school–community connections we had in mind but also reflected CTE goals within the arts, A/V technology, and communications career cluster. The iterative process was contoured by a recurring application of conjectures to each shift in space, resource, and task throughout the school year. The conjectures were as follows: (a) connecting different social spaces extends learning beyond classroom boundaries; (b) providing a range of material, cultural, and human resources creates learning opportunities; and (c) enabling meaningful tasks promotes interest in learning.

The conjectures took into account social categories such as race, ethnicity, class, gender, language, and immigrant status in order to support students' repertoires of cultural practice as assets of learning (Comber and Nixon 2013). This coincided with place as relational and became evident in the data with relation-building processes through which students signaled place-making with the use of media technologies within the learning ecology. Mr. Miles and I attempted to be as inclusive of difference and attentive to students' interests in the arts and technology as possible. To understand these conjectures in context is to understand the high school and CTE of which the multimedia communications class was a part.

School Context within CTE

Randall High School is a comprehensive high school serving racially, ethnically, culturally, and linguistically diverse students, grades 9–12. The high school comprised 76 percent Black, 10.5 percent White, 7.4 percent Asian, and 5.4 percent Hispanic students, inclusive of newly arrived/immigrant students. There were approximately 1,100 students; 74 percent of the student population received free or reduced price lunch (Missouri Department of Elementary and Secondary Education, 2011).

Career and Technical Education

The multimedia communications class at Randall High is situated within CTE's career paths and clusters. Formerly known as vocational education, CTE combines academic standards with career and technical curriculum. In 2012, President Barack Obama reauthorized the Carl D. Perkins Career and Technical Education Act of 2006, a $1.4 billion investment designed to prepare youth and adults to be more "skilled, adaptable, creative, and equipped for success in the global marketplace" (U.S. Department of Education, 2012). Reform plans for CTE utilize incentives and increased autonomy for states that yield high-quality programming and high performance from local recipients. That said, it is important to note that the persisting academic–vocational divide within CTE shapes the schooling experiences of many students. Elsewhere I have argued for the need to rethink CTE and pay attention to alterable conditions in addressing social and educational disparities in students' lives (see Jocson 2015b).

To accept that CTE only produces "high-quality job training opportunities" is to assume students' pathways are straightforward without much room for learning in space-time (Leander, Phillips, and Taylor 2010). It reflects the ongoing academic versus vocational debate that manifests under the guise of "investing in America's future," predetermining what some students are capable of doing by channeling them into particular pathways based on the work of the hand or the brain in school (Rose 2004, 2012, 2014). There remains a belittling of the work and intellectual potential in performing types of learning; that is, the idea that applied learning (as in applied learning in CTE) is mostly useful for those young people who cannot compete academically. This very idea is "destructive and represents a distorted understanding of human ability" (Halpern 2013, 213). In the midst of global economic competition, market-driven forces that insist principally on business growth and employability skills have limited at best the meaning of education to enable human capacity and to benefit the public good.

For the purposes of illuminating place in this chapter, it is important to situate the research as well as the work that students produced as occurring within the context of CTE. Briefly, CTE spans secondary, postsecondary, and adult education levels. At the secondary level, CTE institutional providers are in three main settings: comprehensive high schools offering occupational programs on and off site, full-time CTE high schools, and area CTE schools serving multiple high schools (U.S. Department of Education, 2008). There are sixteen career clusters and programs of study recognized by the Office of Vocational and Adult Education and the National Association of State Directors of Career and Technical Education Consortium (www.careertech.org/career-clusters). Each career cluster comprises career pathways with sequences of academic, career, and technical courses and training to prepare students for transitions from secondary into postsecondary education and the workplace.

The CTE program at Randall High offered seven paths (health, creative, business, nature, helping, building, and fixing); the creative path featured arts, A/V technology, and communications, which includes audio and video technology and film, printing technology, visual arts, performing arts, journalism and broadcasting, and telecommunications (www.missouriconnections.org). The state of Missouri received over $20 million for its CTE programs when this study began in 2010, and served approximately 181,418 secondary students, 80,295 postsecondary students, and 2,626 full-time adults (Missouri Department of Elementary and Secondary Education, 2011).

Mr. Miles and Teaching Multimedia Communications

Despite the silos created by CTE paths and clusters, Mr. Miles built on his former experience as a chemistry teacher and current expertise in information technology to embrace interrelated concepts of problem solving and critical thinking in what he referred to as SMTE (science, math, technology, engineering). He infused SMTE into multimedia

communications. His pedagogical approach exhibited connections between and across career paths such that the creative path (arts, A/V
technology, and communications) was not separate from the business
path (information technology with a focus on network systems) or the
building and fixing paths (science, technology, engineering, and math
with a focus on engineering and technology). In an interview at the beginning of the school year,[5] Mr. Miles noted the "science" of his teaching:

> It's science, math, technology, and engineering. And that's what
> I like because that's what I have identified or recognized as four
> components of problem solving. It's a cycle, a process, of relating
> things. I even call it the "human problem-solving continuum."
> Those four things. Science, you ask a question. Math, you check
> out the connections. Technology, you design a solution, starts off
> virtual and it becomes physical, something tangible. Then engi-
> neering, you create a solution and you bring it into existence . . .
> what I'm saying is that's what I'm looking for when I'm teaching.
> That's what I try to share with students, that learning is a process,
> life is a process.

With his teaching approach, Mr. Miles treated the process of conducting
inquiry projects, producing media, and using technological tools in part
as a learning outcome for students in CTE and also in part as avenues for
addressing issues of inequity in students' lives. Not new to teaching, Mr.
Miles complemented his forty years of working in the classroom with
social activism through an organization focused on the Black struggle.
He was well liked at the school and garnered respect from students; even
students who had graduated came to visit during lunch or after school.

   In our time together during the school year, Mr. Miles and I cultivated
synergy to remain flexible about the dynamics of learning in space-time.
It became evident through observation that Mr. Miles espouses culturally responsive pedagogy and draws on students' cultural strengths as
assets in learning (Gay 2010; Lee 2007). Mr. Miles encouraged students
to pursue their interests in multimedia communications and technology; while doing so, he cast a culture of college and career readiness
aligned with CTE goals through our combined school–university collaboration and larger school–community connections. For Mr. Miles,
multimedia communications is about "problem solving" that draws on

various dimensions of SMTE. This subjective stance influenced my thinking and the ways in which I began to also treat multimedia communications as SMTE.

In the first few weeks of working with Mr. Miles, I began to notice how he was positioning himself in relation to the learning ecology and how he was also positioning his students through a "problem-solving" framework. Such an approach was, of course, relative to the structure of the school as an institution, how the school had positioned Mr. Miles to position his students, and conversely how students had positioned Mr. Miles and themselves as participants within the school. It was not enough for Mr. Miles to create learning opportunities in the multimedia communications classroom (at the computer stations and inside the classroom television studio); Mr. Miles also employed students in school assemblies in the auditorium and sports events during home and away games to extend learning beyond the classroom boundaries. Attending these events *in situ* allowed me as a researcher-collaborator to move across settings and understand the learning ecology as constituted by spaces, resources, and tasks, and vice versa.

To examine the learning ecology of the multimedia communications class, six focal students in the twelfth grade participated in the study. Four identified as African/African American (Carla, Pam, Lamar, and David), one Central American (Celso), and one Southeast Asian (Han); of these students, two identified as female and four identified as male. Students' grade point average ranged from 1.8 to 3.3 on a scale of 4.0. Figure 3 provides a summary of student participants. These students and their work demonstrated the nuances of place-making. With content and visual analysis, themes that emerged led to an understanding of place as relational and contingent upon relationships that are shaped by and constitute people, ideas, and cultures in students' lives (see Appendix B for details on gathering empirical material and the methods and analysis used in this study).

To illuminate place in youth media production, I focus on two instantiations where place as relational (re)positioned students during an initial visit to the school district's television station (first example) and later through media production in the classroom (second example). I emphasize the material and ontological dimensions of place toward place-making as students negotiated ways of relating with each other, their teacher, and other professional staff; with specific places such as

NAME	GENDER	GRADE (AGE)	GPA	EXTRA CURRICULAR	PLANS AFTER HIGH SCHOOL	RACE/ ETHNICITY (SELF-REPORTED)
Carla*	F	12th (18)	2.5		4-year college (Undecided)	African American
Celso	M	12th (19)	1.8	Sports (Baseball)	Work	Central American (Honduran)
David	M	12th (18)	3.0	Sports (Basketball, Track & Field)	4-year college (Undecided)	African American
Han	M	12th (18)	2.4		Work in family business	Southeast Asian (Vietnamese)
Lamar	M	12th (18)	2.5	Sports (Football)	4-year college (Broadcasting or Multimedia)	African American
Pam	F	12th (18)	3.3	Yearbook Conscious Choice Sports (Tennis)	4-year college (Undecided)	African (Togolese)

*Student left CTE in the second semester

FIGURE 3. *Students in Multimedia Communications*

the classroom, community center, and school district television station; and with the technological tools and other resources available in each setting. I offer individual interview, group session, script, and visual data to highlight both place in the research context and place in the presentation of findings.

Learning Ecology as Meeting Place(s)

In creating learning opportunities, Mr. Miles and I considered the following places to make up a learning ecology for multimedia communications: the classroom with computer stations, the classroom television studio with a live set and sound/broadcast booths, the school's auditorium and athletic field, the school district's television station, and a community science resource center serving youth of all ages as well as adults and educators. As I will illustrate, the learning ecology and its constitutive parts established a meeting place (Massey 2005). Noteworthy in learning ecology as meeting place(s) are the material ontologies of place—that is, the different material aspects of media production are already enlivened matter (Barad 2007) shaping students' experience in the high school multimedia communications class.

Drawing on new materialisms, it is important to consider that media technologies are not only inert, prosthetic tools for creating or distributing media texts. They are dynamic matter that can produce and enact ontologies in relation to each other. That is, the camera, computer, television, keyboard, microphone, even trifold poster boards used in the learning ecology serve as mediating tools that enable media texts to be created and distributed (see Figure 4); while delineating what is possible, these media technologies are also used by students through a mutually shaping relationship (Lievrouw 2011). The tool and the experience go hand in hand. Put another way, the materiality of these media technologies is what Barad (2003; 2007) refers to in conceiving matter as already a desiring dynamism, that is, matter is enlivened and enlivening. The materiality of the media technologies is generative and in this case also constitutive of the learning ecology.

CLASSROOM –Computer Stations –Television Studio –Broadcast & Sound Booths		SCHOOL –Auditorium –Athletic Field
	LEARNING ECOLOGY	
SCHOOL DISTRICT BUILDING –Television Studio –Broadcast Office		COMMUNITY CENTER –Presentation Room –Lobby/Exhibit Area

FIGURE 4. *Learning Ecology as Meeting Place(s). Adapted from Jocson 2016a.*

In line with CTE goals to integrate academic and technical knowledge in project-based learning, students in the class were asked to do the following:

1. Create mapping routes using Google Maps and Google Earth (with a focus on school and home);
2. Explore mapping using Social Explorer and GIS mapping (with a focus on Randall High School in a comparative view of other schools and neighborhoods);
3. Watch youth-produced media and local news (with a focus on the city and surrounding area);
4. Identify an educational or social issue for a PSA, slideshow, and op-ed video (with a focus on home-school-neighborhood-city-surrounding area).

In each instance, place was key to completing the task. An example of a group session at the school district television station illuminates how the material ontologies of place produced and enacted possibilities for students' place-making, and how place-making was contingent upon relationships.

After completing the mapping exercises and showcasing student work at the community center, arrangements were made for the multimedia communications class to also utilize the school district television station situated in the school district office building. The school district's television station, approximately a ten-minute ride from the high school, provided students opportunities to work side-by-side with the professional staff. The station consisted of a live studio set and broadcast booth with industry standard equipment; there were two professional male staff whose office workspace was located adjacent to the studio.

An introductory group session illustrates how the material ontologies of place are generative and mutually constitutive in place-making. In the following excerpt, the station's professional staff, Mr. Collin and Mr. Bender, welcomed the students visiting for the first time and identified various aspects of the studio. All six students, Mr. Miles, Mr. Collin, and Mr. Bender sat in a semicircle in the studio's live set. Mr. Miles opened the dialogue. Noteworthy in the exchange is how place as enlivened and enlivening matter (re)arranges what is possible for youth as participants and media producers. This is displayed in **bold** text below.

MR. MILES: Thanks for having us. We're glad to be here. I'm [Miles] here with some awesome students.

(students share their names)

MR. COLLIN: Welcome. It's good to have you here. This is the staff. My name is [Collin]. This is [Bender]. . . We've probably created three or four thousand original productions in the ten years we've been here. Right now we're producing a news program called *Spotlight News*. We cover a lot of the various district events. We spent a lot of time in the last year promoting schools throughout the district . . . so, that's been a major part of what we've been doing lately. In this studio, we have three cameras. They're all standard definition. We've got a teleprompter. **As you can see, we've got lighting grids. You all are sitting on our set, which can be rearranged in a lot of different ways.** We took components of our old set and just tried to sort of integrate everything together, but we have two sets in this studio space that can be configured in different ways.

(overlapping)

MR. BENDER: Well, actually three, I guess, with the green screen.

MR. COLLIN: Yeah, with the green screen.

MR. BENDER: **So we've got the green screen, there on the side, and this gray background behind us for simple headshots and interview pieces,** and then the rest of the set for more elaborate shows.

MR. COLLIN: So actually we've got four because we've got the one [in the back] with the blue panels that also has interchangeable panels. . . So we've got the basis for some creativity.

MR. BENDER: We kind of have to set up [around] the lighting patterns, and we [basically] have three different arrangements for the lights. If we want to change it, it's a little more trouble to rearrange or reposition lights. **So we pretty much have it so we can do any of those set ups with very little changing of the lighting grids.** It makes it easier when there's just two of us.

LAMAR: Is the room soundproof?

MR. COLLIN: Yeah, we can close the door.

As the session continued, students became more verbal and asked specific questions. Lamar, Carla, Pam, and David chimed in. By doing so, these students were inserting themselves into the group session and were beginning to embrace the television station as a platform for producing media and sharing it with a public audience. Questions about equipment doubly served as a way to signal place-making.

LAMAR: How do you teleprompt?

MR. BENDER: *(standing up)* Well, it works off this computer, **so I have controls here. It scrolls at different speeds so that the talent can read off of this *(points to camera)*.** And that's what I usually do with *Spotlight News* . . . I'll have a host who reads news pieces or intro pieces or is conducting an interview live. **There's text to sequence the program and that comes off of here, so that makes it easier. The person has to look straight in here,** essentially looking straight at anybody watching the program. That, you know, takes practice.

(overlapping)

LAMAR: So you don't have to look off to the side or nothing?

CARLA: What if . . .

(overlapping)

MR. BENDER: . . . right, **the person is looking at you.**

CARLA: What if the person can't see the teleprompter?

MR. BENDER: Well . . .

(overlapping)

MR. COLLIN: . . . we move it closer.

MR. BENDER: Or make the text larger. Or push the camera in closer, if we need to.

CARLA: Oh, ok. That's good. **That's better for me.**

(silence)

MR. COLLIN: Not to worry. Hopefully you won't need to rely on the teleprompter, except maybe for the open, or close, or breaks initially. Because hopefully, you know, conversation would drive the show.

CARLA: **Yeah, that's what we're working on.**

MR. COLLIN: So, I got a question. What do you all want to do? What is your project?

LAMAR: Um, our project, **we want to show where we stand on the map. Like, we want to show people how things are, our lives . . . like the project we just did,** different routes we take going to school and stuff. What we encounter . . . things that happen and stuff.

PAM: **And we also want to locate the graduates.** People who have already graduated from [our high school]. **Where they at right now, what they doing and stuff, and like making sure they put us on the map.**

DAVID: **That's the topic I'm interested in.** We talked about it in class.

MR. COLLIN: So, once you locate some of these graduates, um, how will you get their input? I mean, **how will you interview them, or would you contact them and have them come to the studio, or you going to go to them?**

DAVID: Um, **probably do it over the phone,** or if they got time, **they can come down and talk to us.**

MR. COLLIN: What will the show look like?

LAMAR: It'd be your standard set, desk, and stuff. Green screen. It's just going to be a lot of little things we put together. Like different, like on the green screen we have the person's face and what they did to get to college.

The idea to feature graduates links to work students had done in the classroom prior to visiting the television studio. Mapping exercises had prompted their thinking about schools and neighborhoods, and issues of equity in education. The material ontologies of place in the television station were continuing to shape their project. "Put Us on the Map" (a title selected by students themselves) was about being in dialogue with the public and leaving behind an alternative view of young people. Evident below is how students began to treat place as relational based on the work they envisioned in producing and showing where they figuratively "stand on the map."

MR. COLLIN: So, basically the process they went through to accomplish whatever their current situation is.

LAMAR: Yeah. **We're doing it so that we can bring it to the freshmen, the upperclassmen and all that.**

MR. COLLIN: Who do you want to see the program when it's complete? Who is it being created for?

PAM: **We want the [city] to see it, so they can see what the young people are doing.** Instead of just hanging out on the street and the bad stuff on TV all the time. They can see what good things happened too.

MR. COLLIN: Yeah, I can see that. **And that's one of the first things whenever you work on any kind of media project. You want to ask, what is the end result going to be? Who am I creating this for?** Because that will dictate the technology you need to use in order to accomplish your goal.

LAMAR: Yeah. We kind of did that in class. **The news don't give a full picture. We want to interview students like us.**

MR. BENDER: Ok. **What about interview pieces? Are those the pieces that you would want to do in here [the studio]?** And then it sounds like a lot of the other video might be out in the field that you would shoot?

PAM: **That's something we're still figuring out. I guess we can do some in the studio or take the camera out.**

MR. MILES: **Last year the seniors did that and produced some awesome commercials.** And they all bragged about them. **You all got to step that game up. So talk about putting [the school's name] on the map.**

MR. COLLIN: Ok, so when you get the rhythm of coming down here, then I'm sure everybody will open up and feel more comfortable. 'Cause you know, **the bottom line is, this is your studio. You belong down here.**

In subsequent visits to the television station, students with a better grasp of available tools and resources in the television station did seem to be a bit more comfortable. This led to taking on particular roles. Lamar and Carla agreed to be behind the camera as technicians and operators; Pam, along with David, agreed to be in front of the camera as anchors and hosts. Two other students, Han and Celso, who were not verbal in the initial visit, claimed the roles of floor director and sound-broadcast engineer, respectively. They had been making beats in school, on their own or with other students, and tended to be behind the scenes of production. In all, as highlighted here, the school district television station as part of the larger learning ecology served as a meeting place that created learning opportunities for students to become active media producers using standard industry equipment. The Put Us on the Map project was underway.

Put Us on the Map: Place and Call to Action

In line with CTE goals, students as members of arts, A/V technology, and communications were expected to advance their academic-technical knowledge, and thus were tasked to create a television broadcast. Mr. Miles encouraged students to think of the Put Us on the Map project as an opportunity not only to immerse in digital media technology but also to promote dialogue and raise awareness about an educational or social issue they deemed significant in their lives. In an interview, Mr. Miles noted how the project is tied to his teaching philosophy and to media production that treats place as relational:

> I believe in enabling, creating a learning environment where people can try out things, and it's ok to make mistakes. That's part of learning. It's ok to be honest and open. To me, that's key. Listen to people . . . [because] when you really listen, then we can tailor learning to our own purposes. And that's what this project is about. I want students to be able to tell their own story, and to listen to other people's stories, and use the digital tools we have to allow that . . .Digital video applications like iMovie, digital photo and music applications like iPhoto, iTunes, and GarageBand. Of course, there are others from basic to advanced. For broadcasting, there's Videocue and Wirecast that we now have in our studio. You know, all of these are tools for digital storytelling now in everyday people's hands. Technology has been democratized. That's important to career and technical education.

With this in mind, Mr. Miles set out to create learning opportunities as part of the learning ecology and worked with students individually and collectively in preparation for the Put Us on the Map project.

Scaffolding was important to the learning process. Mr. Miles began with a mean-dog exercise, where students described the routes they took to/from school (by foot, by bike, by car, or by bus), identified specific places in their neighborhoods where barking or aggressive dogs were located, and noted whether they altered their routes because of the dogs. Students were familiar with global positioning systems (GPS) but not so familiar with geographic information systems (GIS). The mean-dog exercise included mapping specific locations using Google Maps with Google Earth set for different planes of view. From there, Mr. Miles proceeded with a mapping exercise, this time mapping particular cultural and educational institutions such as libraries and museums.

Through the school–university partnership, Mr. Miles drew on a free database with information on fifty-seven school districts in the metropolitan area that allowed students to use GIS to explore the relationship between schools and neighborhoods. At the university, I accessed the same database in an undergraduate-level course studying literacy-rich environments, including community-based organizations with literacy or technology programs (see Jocson and Thorne-Wallington 2013). At this point our partnership led us to a community science resource center in order to manifest school–community connections and collectively showcase the work of both high school and college students there. That is to say, Mr. Miles and I did not just arrive at the Put Us on the Map project without serious consideration of learning opportunities through school–community connections enabled by notions of place as relational.

In the Put Us on the Map project, topics selected by students were high school graduation rates, poverty and unemployment, teen pregnancy, gang violence, and drugs.[6] Below, I highlight the work of two students, Celso and Pam, to illustrate their call to action as a form of place-making. The PSA scripts and recorded segments forming the basis of the op-ed video demonstrate rich literate repertoires; more than that, they signify how Celso and Pam see themselves or are making sense of their place in the world.

Language and Audience in Media Production: Celso's Case

Celso selected gang violence and the internationalization of gang affiliation as a topic. He used images found on the Internet as background to go along with the green screen. Celso, who is bilingual in English and Spanish, chose to record and broadcast his multimedia project entirely in Spanish with no English subtitles. As he noted in an interview, "Spanish felt right" to reach a targeted audience. The choice was purposeful and reflected the embrace of a particular communicative logic. I present the following excerpt in the Spanish language, as he did in his script.

> *Hola, mi nombre es [Celso]. Soy un estudiante de [Randall High School].*
> *Del tema que voy a hablar es pandillas y violencia en el mundo y como*
> *afectan a nosotros los estudiantes hoy en día.*
> *. . . Mi pregunta es, ¿Quién va a parar la violencia? ¿Cuando vamos*
> *a entender que tenemos que hacer algo?*
> *. . . Es tiempo de empezar de cambiar. Es tiempo de empezar a ver*
> *hechos y no palabras. ¿Cómo tu quieres tu futuro?¿Quieres vivir toda*
> *tu vida como un prisionero?¿Cómo tu quieres? Yo no quiero este futuro*
> *para mi o para mis hijos. Te invito que me ayudes a luchar contra este*
> *problema.*
> *. . . La vida solo es una. Aprendela, vivirla.*

Indeed, it is time for change. Celso in the broadcast was asking what it takes to create change and makes a plea for action, to value, learn, and live life (loose translation). In an interview describing his topic selection, he revealed:

> When I came here [a couple of years ago] from New York, before
> that, Honduras, I was basically involved in [stuff] so I think my
> main thing now is trying to focus on the young people. . . . TV, like
> the streets, got two faces, the good face and the bad face. . . . I'm just
> trying to give young people a message 'cause I already learned from
> my past. So now I'm trying to teach other people about what I passed
> through . . . 'cause programs on TV don't really show the real thing.

Celso was using the project as a platform to voice his concern for future generations. He added:

I have four younger brothers and I don't want them to pass through what I passed through. I know a lot of folks who pass through more things than me, more troubles than me, but I think I can do my part. My mom came to the U.S. when I was one year old. I lived with my grandpa in Honduras until I was thirteen. I was in New York with my mom before we moved here. I was hanging out and partying, getting into trouble. I can't do it no more.

Celso's place-making as represented in his script and op-ed video crosses geographic boundaries as well as linguistic–cultural borders (Anzaldúa 1987; Massey 2005). He signals place not only according to his personal experience but also via material ontologies of place in the photographs of (inter)national gangs included in his slideshow. He acknowledged that the selection of particular images was deliberate, in an effort to reach his target audience, because, as he said, "TV don't really show the real thing." The notion of place as relational became apparent with Celso recalling his relationship with people he hung out with, his relationship with his mother, grandfather, and siblings, and his relationship to his new environment. The recall became less about finding fault and more about the lessons learned in projecting a possible future. To complete the op-ed video, Celso worked in class, during lunch, and on Saturday sessions when Mr. Miles opened up the classroom for students. There were cycles of writing and revision in the process, followed by the recording of the script using the teleprompter.

Language and Popular Culture in Media Production: Pam's Case

Like Celso, Pam selected a meaningful topic. She had been a member of the Conscious Choice mentoring program at school and was interested in featuring teen pregnancy in the Put Us on the Map project. She used images found on the Internet as background for the green screen and also created a slideshow with recording artist Rihanna's 2006 song "Unfaithful" playing in the background. For Pam, this stylistic choice built on a popular song in order to draw audience attention to her topic. Pam is bilingual in English and Gbe languages, and the use of images and song was purposeful for emphatic effect. In script form, Pam wrote the following excerpt:

Hello, my name is [Pam] and I am a senior at [Randall High School]. My topic is teenage pregnancy. As a seventeen year old with plans to attend college, I feel it is my responsibility to talk about why teenage pregnancy is a huge issue for many girls and young women.

. . . Did you know that by the age of fifteen, 20 percent of girls and 30 percent of boys in the U.S. are sexually active?

. . . [This] is why I encourage you to talk to the teens in your communities and see how you can support girls and young women as they go through this important stage in their lives. Help us help the future generation.

I'm sharing a slideshow on the topic of teenage pregnancy as a member of Conscious Choice. I encourage you to watch it and ask yourself how you can help. Thank you.

Like Celso, Pam was expressing her concern for a particular issue and the need for collective action. She had joined Conscious Choice the year before to add to other extracurricular activities such as the senior council and the soccer team. Pam noted:

> I'm a strong believer in standing up for what you believe in. This topic [of teenage pregnancy] is about that, being informed and making good choices. To me, it's like putting my future, my education, first. There's nothing wrong with delaying having kids . . . for example, if I get pregnant now, that would mean I'd stop school to get a job and take care of the baby. Personally, I'd rather wait. My sister is in that situation right now. She's twenty-two and got pregnant when she was a senior. . . . Well, I have a nephew who's cute and everything but it makes you see how hard it is to take care of everything . . . she keeps putting off college.

Pam's place-making is apparent. Her parents moved to the United States from Togo with expectations that their children would pursue higher education. Pam was drawing on personal experience to take up the topic of teen pregnancy. Pam's script and recorded segment were both shaped by notions of place as relational and contingent upon relationships, in this case, Pam's relationship with her sister, her nephew, and the Conscious Choice mentoring program. Her call to action builds on literate repertoires further enabled by the material ontologies of place to speak to a larger audience through the use of digital tools in the new media landscape.

Rewriting and Place-Making

"Put Us on the Map" was broadcast through the school television network, where students like Celso and Pam were (re)writing themselves in their own terms. They were delineating what is possible (or not) through their own lived experiences, with concern for the next generation. They were, in relation to each other, marking *their* place in history. This is an important social consequence of media production, particularly in an era of gentrification, hyper-isolation, alienation, and the disposability of youth (Giroux 2012). Students' calls to action are effectively a call to confront social invisibility, a response to neoliberal standardization of education that presents pedagogical possibilities for integrating learning, literacy, and technology with place-based media production. In the spring semester that followed, students revisited this project with extended scripts and recorded segments created at the school district television station as part of their internship. The following school year, another iteration of place-based media production allowed a different set of students to choose different topics to pursue within and across the learning ecology.

Linking Place, Learning Ecology, and Literacy

The analysis of learning ecology as meeting place(s), as well as the discussion of the Put Us on the Map project, point to the value of rethinking place beyond the "local" spatial boundaries of the classroom, school, and neighborhood. Building on conceptualizations of place and the combined works of interdisciplinary scholars, place-based media production must account for difference, boundary, and connectivity in students' lives that may be influenced by new materialist manifestations of ecology where the dynamics of space, time, and matter are considered across local–global boundaries (Barad 2007; Massey 2005). This has been the case for Celso and Pam, whose (im)migrant experiences render place as contingent upon relationships with family and friends that shaped the topics selected (and stories constructed) for the Put Us on the Map project. Moreover, the dynamism in the material ontologies of place considers how students are individually and collectively connected to place and how media technologies within the learning ecology are enlivened matter that highlight that dynamic relationship.

The study's findings suggest place-based media production as integral to teaching and learning in ways that support students' interests in the arts and technology, that is, seeing students not as passive consumers but as active producers of knowledge. Place-based media production offered opportunities for weaving students' lives into their learning in the service of place-making. This is important, as students are in the process of becoming, making sense of their place and making a place in the world. Place-based media production delineated pedagogical possibilities for students to face familiar and unfamiliar aspects of multimedia communications as a domain of learning in which they constructed relational experiences as racialized, gendered, and minoritized youth in order to enter, alter, and/or disrupt dominant discourses of educational and social issues affecting their lives. The integration of academic and technical knowledge in place-based media production was crucial for innovating pedagogical practices in CTE. There were opportunities for developing students' literate repertoires as well as for building on their tacit knowledge and cultural practices.

Thus, in linking place and learning ecology to literacy, educators must consider notions of place as relational and situated within trans-local networks in the fullness of youth's lives—from *what* and *when* they write, with/for *whom*, and *where* they access a range of places in the process of becoming through participation and engagement with digital media technology. This is crucial for both research and practice, particularly in the area of literacy studies where PBE has been influential in curriculum and instruction. From what I have tried to illustrate here, it should be evident that place is more than a backdrop. Place is integral to engineering forms of learning (i.e., learning ecology) and innovating pedagogical practices that draw on issues of difference and place-making toward educative possibilities. Place-based media production in the context of CTE specifically and education more broadly offers new contributions to education research. For me and Mr. Miles, there were many lessons to shape the next multimedia communications class.

What Happened the Following School Year

Five focal students (all students of color) participated in the study the second year. Featured below are three students and their multimedia projects.[7] Similar to the previous year, the study was specific to multimedia communications as part of the arts, A/V technology, and communications career cluster. In a project exploring community issues, twelfth-grade African American female student Ally partnered with a biracial African American–White female student Michelle to focus on sexual health. Ally conveyed the following about their topic, its significance, and what was involved in the production:

> I liked it. The information was good. My project was with [Michelle] on sex education and STDs. Well, for me, I felt it was necessary to do that topic because I live in [zip code] and that's the one with the highest rates for STDs among young adults here so I felt it was important. And a lot of times, well, I can say they really don't teach sex education anymore and why not? I feel like, if they did, then children around my age and older would make wiser decisions and the rate of STDs wouldn't be so high as it is. . . . When [the teacher] introduced us to this project and started speaking about different things we could do, that was exciting . . . [Michelle] and I used Google Earth and Social Explorer maps . . . we did research on websites to get information, statistics, and then put everything together, recording it. . . . It was scary and fun at the same time. It felt good.

The outcome of the process described above was a short video. During my time in this multimedia communications class, I came to understand that Ally and Michelle's concerns regarding sexual health expressed in the video were also shared by other students in a mentoring program called Conscious Choice. Pam from the previous school year, a former member of Conscious Choice, also emphasized the importance of sex education in her multimedia project. For Ally (and Michelle), it was important to utilize the multimedia communications class project as another platform for promoting awareness about sexual health that affected young people's lives. The production of the video reflects analytical thinking and synthesis with a public audience in mind.

The topics selected by students in this multimedia communications class ranged from sexual health to racial diversity and public parks with an emphasis on community issues that students deemed vital to their everyday lives. Hagi, a twelfth-grade female African immigrant student from Kenya, chose the topic of racial and cultural diversity to raise awareness about the experiences of many students like her at the school. In a previous assignment, Hagi wrote about learning the English language and the experience of feeling isolated and without many friends due to language barriers. She spoke Somali and Swahili and, according to her, it was difficult to communicate with many of her teachers at first. At the time of the study, Hagi maintained a 3.2 grade point average and had submitted applications to three four-year state universities with hopes of studying health sciences. Hagi was involved in various after school activities, including the Fashion Club and an ACT preparation class; she also participated in a local dance studio, attended health sciences informational sessions at a nearby university hospital, and joined college-going workshops in school. Hagi shared the following about her project in the multimedia communications class:

> People at the school see us wearing different clothes but they don't know where we come from or who we are. . . there are a lot of students, international students, and I see it every single day, . . . I come to school [and] I see people around me, how they treat each other, and in the cafeteria how they have different groups and stuff. So I thought I should write about that to help, you know. When I decided I was going to do it, I used Social Explorer and census data sites to look up information on people living in the area. I also interviewed students and then after that put the whole thing together. Some stuff I didn't know how to do but I learned and enjoyed doing the project.

Similarly, twelfth-grade African American male student Marlon explained the importance of selecting parks and recreation as a topic. Marlon partnered with Wendell, a fellow twelfth-grade African American male student, to produce a video that demonstrated connective threads between parks and recreation, safety, and health; both were curious about the viability of public spaces where teens could go and hang out. They used Google Maps and Social Explorer to visualize the metropolitan area's public parks, but in this process of inquiry they also became specifically interested in recreational centers and landed on websites of organizations that focused on child and adolescent health. Upon researching information online, their initial idea of parks and recreation led them to thinking about the health and well-being of young people. Marlon noted insights gained from the production:

> [The project] was about health issues and safety basically. . . . not a lot of us go to the park because it's not safe, kind of like how sometimes we have to take a different way to school to avoid stuff, you know, or just be picked up and dropped off. This project was new to me. . . . I did the script and did a little research myself, and [Wendell] looked up information too. I learned some new things, yeah, like the obesity rate stood out for me. I didn't know it was that high for people our age. It made me think about how kids are participating or not participating in activities outside of school. The other projects connected with ours like [Ally and Michelle's]. The connections were interesting. Kind of mind blowing, I thought.

Marlon completed the video with Wendell in a timely fashion despite demands of his part-time job. At the time of the study, Marlon was unsure about his immediate post-secondary plans. He maintained a 3.1 grade point average, yet was undecided on college. Marlon was keen on taking a break from school in order to focus on life priorities before, as he said, "going to college sometime the following year." Such examples of students' participation in multimedia communications as linked to their various interests and pathways to post-secondary education or the workplace reveal a different understanding of how CTE as a learning domain can open up avenues for possible futures. This understanding also marks the importance of place in youth media production. The focus on school- and community-based issues such as sexual health, racial and cultural diversity, and recreational opportunities tells us that students are delineating what *can be* to better the circumstances that shape their lives. Place-making is key to youth media.

Advancing Place in Theory and Research

It is important to consider some limitations of place-based media production. The first limitation relates to the conceptualization of place as tied to a learning ecology. Some conjectures grounded the research and led me and Mr. Miles to take a particular approach. As well, Mr.

Miles and I maintained focus on settings that directly related to CTE's career cluster of arts, A/V technology, and communications (i.e., classroom and classroom television studio, school auditorium and athletic field, community science resource center, and school district television station). For us, these settings emphasized possibilities for engineering and studying forms of learning through multimedia communications and technology that may be distinct from other contexts.

A second limitation relates to generalization. Randall High School and the school district are situated in the urban Midwest. While CTE reaches many schools and school districts, what I have shared in the discussion speaks to a particular place, space, time, and matter. It is my hope that the examination of place-based media production in this particular multimedia communications classroom and learning ecology provides an example for advancing the conversation, especially in light of Common Core State Standards (CCSS) implementation and college and career readiness within CTE. Many states have adopted CCSS, yet CTE with its integration of academic and occupational knowledge as well as technical skills remains an understudied area.

A third limitation relates to methodology. The ethnography was shaped by an agreed upon partnership mainly between one CTE teacher and one university researcher-collaborator who not only emphasized place, but also employed design-based research to shape the learning ecology toward particular forms of learning. Visual and conventional ethnographic methods served as a means for documenting and analyzing place. The flow from one specific place to another—crossing the spatial boundaries in the learning ecology—necessitated participant observations as well as the use of a still camera to try to capture moments *in situ*. Thus, additional methods such as videotaping, multiple researchers within and across the learning ecology, and data analytics on websites visited by students while conducting online search for their select topics can be helpful to document movements, shifting dynamics in place, and the use of digital media technology when students are working on their own or in small groups.

What Now?

In anticipating possibilities in research and practice, it might be worthwhile to think of place or the material ontologies of place as connected to learning. Perhaps even *as* connected learning. An agenda for research on digital media and learning proposes a model that allows for reimagining education in the information age (Ito et al. 2013). This model is helpful to rethink what we do in education in ways that attend to young people's interests and passions with the support of friends and caring adults; through this approach, learning is seen as connected to social, academic, career, and life trajectories. A previous gathering of digital media and learning scholars focused on an important theme of "equity by design" to address issues of difference and inequities in education. It featured examples of connected learning taking place in "hives" and pushed for more ways to understand "cities of learning" as a new initiative. It seems that notions of place as relational, as a constellation of trajectories, and as connected to learning can offer new directions in research, design, and implementation.

As I continue to think about my own work, I am further challenged by how and why place matters in understanding literacy, learning, and youth media production. Processes of becoming at the very least must consider the material ontologies of place and place-making. The topic of land and Indigenous connections to land must be a part of such processes, particularly because educational and social issues raised by young people are linked to the current rhetoric and practices of nativity, anti-immigration, and anti-blackness. Unraveling the complexity of settler colonialism can provide a lens for further examining place and place-making in youth media. The changing dynamics of space, time, and matter move the thinking away from the politics of location to the politics of place and pedagogies of possibility.

Place-based media production as presented in this chapter builds on place as a multidisciplinary construct. Educators are increasingly interested in drawing on place-based approaches to innovate pedagogical practices. Within literacy studies, place has been one way to understand and further develop the literate repertoires of students from varied social and cultural backgrounds. Critical inquiry conducted by students, within a learning ecology involving partners in education, can bring forth new questions about future designs of school–university partnerships with an eye toward critical place inquiry (Tuck and McKenzie 2015). Such pedagogical possibilities of place are key for connecting partners in education with an expanded social imagination. Embracing a range of students' relational experiences can offer a tangible means of understanding the world, as well as how students (re)construct it to make a difference. The next chapter focuses on youth media as pedagogy and the ways in which social action projects created by college students blur the lines between cultural production and participatory politics.

4

Centrality of Pedagogy in the College Classroom

The semester began a bit on the rough side. I was slated to teach a course with a focus on new media literacies and yet it took three different class-rooms to find the right one. My students and I shuffled every week for three weeks before we could decide which space would be conducive to the kinds of activities described on the syllabus. Finally, with support from a colleague who was also a university librarian, a meeting room with a podium, movable tables, booths, a whiteboard, and a drop-down projector was assigned to us for temporary use inside the main campus library. My students and I were happy for the time being. Then, when our critical feedback reached the library's administrative head, we were moved to an "active learning" classroom adjacent to that meeting room. The spatial flexibility afforded by the swivel desk chairs turned out to be important to us. The classroom had an interactive Smart Board, a document camera, and a computer media panel to accommodate our needs. The classroom was also equipped with Wi-Fi connectivity and four iMac computer stations. As noted in the previous chapter, the ma-terial ontologies of place are mutually constitutive and enable media production in particular ways. They certainly mattered to us and the kinds of things we hoped to accomplish in a semester-long course.

This chapter draws on my own teaching to offer insights on youth media as pedagogy. To be clear, pedagogy strives toward different modes of understanding. Pedagogy is a deliberate attempt to influence how and what knowledge and identities are produced to create experiences that help to organize and disorganize how we understand the world and so-cial relations in it (Giroux and Simon 1989). I focus on a course that theorized and practiced new media literacies. In what follows, I discuss curricular components incorporating students' own new media litera-cies at work. Specific activities and assignments took place inside and outside of the classroom. Students enrolled in this course (ages 19–25) were asked to participate in a class blog (viewable by the public) as one way to share responses to readings, facilitate an in-class discussion with a partner using multimedia tools, create a digital story, and produce a short documentary along with an interactive website. For the latter, students were asked to examine a particular educational or social issue that would raise awareness about a historically segregated city in the urban Midwest. The resultant social action projects (video documentaries and interactive websites) served as an example of engaging in the politics of knowledge production. Additionally, I provide a discussion on the use of producer's commentary to better understand students' digital stories and further guide the course leading up to the social action projects.

Building on my previous ethnographic studies, I espoused a design-based approach to learning in order to be theory-oriented, iterative, interventionist, and pragmatic (Cobb et al. 2003). I also borrowed from action research, a form of teacher inquiry, for the work to be cyclical, contextual, ethical, and reflective in the pursuit of learning and change (Cochran-Smith and Lytle 1993; 1999; McIntyre 2008). This is important to mention because my students and I did not just arrive with set plans for the social action projects conducted at the end of the semester. Designing curriculum necessitated careful attention to cohort and context (Luke, Woods, and Weir 2013). This meant situating ourselves during our time together within the sociopolitical context of the university and the larger community.[1] This also meant co-constructing a learning space where varied resources and materials (official and unofficial) would come together in support of our purpose and needs. To that end, new media literacies as a course topic served as the context through which to explore participatory politics and issues of public concern that we as a cohort constructed together.

Participatory Politics and New Media Literacies

Today's creative expressions blur the lines between youth cultural production and participatory politics. There are myriad ways of participating in civic life. Many young people around the world are drawing on new media literacies and popular culture to make videos, take photographs, create websites, write blogs, assemble mash-ups, and share their creations online for others to view (Williams and Zenger 2012). From a new media literacies perspective, it is argued that an ethos of collaboration, participation, and distributed expertise shapes how individuals see themselves in the world and interact with each other through digital technologies (Lankshear and Knobel 2006). At the center of this onto-logical and technocultural shift are youths who engage in alternative and activist practices (Lievrouw 2011).

Such practices reflect what Cohen et al. (2012) call participatory politics, in which interactive, peer-based acts have the ability to reach large audiences, shape agendas through dialogue, and exert greater agency through the circulation of information and the production of original content—both online and offline. In this light, the notion of participatory politics is seen as wielding voice and influence on issues of public concern without being guided by deference to elites or formal institutions. Participatory politics are interest-driven and voluntary. In my continued work with secondary and tertiary students, I have been moved by the potential of participatory politics not only as voluntary, but also as pedagogically operational in critical education (Anyon 2009a; 2009b; Apple, Au, and Gandin 2009).

What happens when participatory politics become a key component of the classroom experience? What pedagogical considerations are nec-essary to enable both students and educators to embrace varied uses of technology toward alternative and activist practices? In what ways can the curriculum be invigorated by interest-driven and peer-based acts within the confines of school, university, and other formal institutions? Philip and Garcia (2013) remind us of the centrality of pedagogy and the continued need for a dynamic relationship between students and teach-ers in supporting today's iGeneration. What I describe in this chapter is an instantiation of youth cultural production and participatory politics in the context of a new media literacies (NML) course. Given the pace of changing technologies and changing practices, it is important to exam-ine specific ways through which youth leverage new media literacies in order to understand pedagogical possibilities.

As the instructor of record, I positioned myself as a learning partner open to ideas and suggestions; with that goal in mind, class sessions took a seminar format. Ultimately a public screening and exhibit was held at a nearby museum to showcase student work. The event was de-liberate in order to promote dialogue across institutional spaces and to further legitimize youth voice and influence on local matters (Cohen et al. 2012; Soep and Chávez 2010; Soep 2014). Noteworthy in the course was an ethos that developed through *collaboration, participation,* and *dis-tributed expertise* leading to the production of video documentaries and interactive websites. Multilayered and occurring across off- and online spaces, the inquiry and media-making processes built on a set of new media literacies such as play, transmedia navigation, and visualization (Jenkins 2006a)[2]. These new media literacies served as core cultural competencies and social skills in a new media landscape, but more important emerged as key practices toward youth cultural production and participatory politics.

Moreover, these new media literacies coincided with exciting ideas about connected learning. Concerned with the changing demands of learning as noted in the previous chapter, I found it important to draw on what Ito and colleagues (2013) call a model of connected learning, which fuses learning principles (youth's interests, peer culture, and academic achievement) with design principles (hands-on production, shared purpose, and open networks). Driving this model of connected learning are core values of equity, full participation, and social connection. Together, the learning principles, design principles, and core values of connected learning reflected for me possibilities in the classroom, which in the case of our classroom were centered on the conceptualization and application of new media literacies.

In short, the uncertainty in the inquiry opened up opportunities for students and me to collaboratively recognize the value of new media literacies in everyday life and new media literacies as a form of social action toward a (re)interpretation of lived and constructed realities. The insights shared here point to the centrality of pedagogy in the politics of knowledge production. To understand youth media as pedagogy, let me turn now to the work of students.

Doing the Work in/with New Media Literacies

Social action projects were the culmination of the course. We got there via different aspects of the learning process, including course readings, discussions (in class and online), and various assignments. A deliberate shift took place in week four from theory building to the practice of new media literacies. Several questions guided our initial conversations. What are forms of new media? What is new or different about them? What are we doing in our lives that helps to constitute new media literacies in the digital era? At times, there were debatable points such as video chatting or reading an e-book. That is, the act of communicating or reading seemed to be the same but the technology in question was different or the ways in which that technology shaped the person's ontological experience was different. We turned to our course readings for additional perspectives (Lankshear and Knobel 2006; Lister et al. 2009). Of course, we were also enacting forms of new media literacies throughout the semester. Activities and assignments such as blogging, group presentations, experiential learning poster project, and digital story are described below.

Blogging

A class blog served as our discussion canvas. Responses based on weekly readings were shared on the blog. For organizational purposes, I posted a visual (as opposed to written) prompt consisting of figurative images under the appropriate topic heading each week. The idea was to be suggestive and not be prescriptive about the reader-response approach to the assigned readings. Students used the blog as an opportunity to comment on what they found most striking about the readings; sometimes, students contested or critiqued statements previously posted by their peers. A minimum of five substantive entries per student was required for the semester. Open to the public, the class blog was meant to encourage students to write with a broader audience in mind, and to think of the online discussion as one way to contribute to the larger discourse on new media literacies.

Group Presentations

Aside from online discussions, activities and assignments throughout the course encouraged students to be dialogic, collaborative, and exploratory. Based on class enrollment, I preselected a number of readings for the purpose of group presentations. Thirteen students signed up to work in pairs for a total of six groups and one solo presenter (a graduate student); each group prepared summary points with the use of PowerPoint or Prezi slides. As it turned out, the class blog served as a resource with comments posted the night before a group presentation. Students facilitating the group presentation were responsible for monitoring blog comments for further discussion in class. As a common practice, I read all of the blog comments before each class session to see the level of engagement and to keep up with patterns in students' thinking. Each group presentation took on a seminar format where class members, including myself, sat around in a semicircle. The swivel chairs enabled us to move around. Each group presentation included a contemporary multimedia example (typically a video from YouTube) to incite thinking about the topic at hand; there were instances when small group activities (i.e., quick online search, think-pair-share, interactive performance) were embedded in the group presentation. Several students typically had their own laptops or smart phones available to use for related activities.

Experiential Learning Poster Project

As we moved toward weeks five to eight of the semester, different articles and studies of new media literacies in youth's lives provided practical insights (Ito 2010; Palfrey and Gasser 2008; Scott and White 2011). Genres of participation such as hanging out, messing around, and geeking out offered a framework for us to consider. By connecting theory to practice across contexts, students pointed out the permeability and nonlinearity in the genres; that is, they recognized that today's participatory culture is bidirectionally shaped by the availability of do-it-yourself digital media technologies and by the participants who tinker with them as creators and learners. The notion of messing around or tinkering with digital media technologies, which to an extent draws on elements of play, transmedia navigation, and negotiation, was helpful to our growing understanding of new media literacies. This also became an important lens through which to examine what happens in different technology-rich environments such as museums, libraries, coffee shops, the Apple store, and even the metro or subway train.

   As part of an experiential learning exercise, students visited "technology-rich" environments and their observations led to a group analysis, including but not limited to technology and public access, spatial design, portability, mobility, and connectivity. The class divided up into eight groups; each group produced a poster with general information and analysis, including representative artifacts and visual images of the technology-rich environment. The theories and practices of new media literacies we had been discussing complemented specific observations. For example, students reported that technology-rich environments were "rich" due in part to the material and human resources that allow for digitally mediated interactions and networked activities (Ito, 2010; Ito et al. 2013; Lister et al. 2009). Students also noted the variability in spatial design conducive to specific purposes, including physical setups for messing around as an element of learning. What seemed to be emerging at this stage in the course was attention to sociocultural dimensions of new media literacies, in ways that also tied to the new technical stuff and new ethos stuff that had been previously discussed.

Digital Story

The notion of messing around (which we adopted as tinkering with digital media technologies) remained central in the course as students engaged in hands-on production. The digital story project was purposeful for working with specific media editing tools. For eleven out of the thirteen students, media production was a new experience. I began to notice that tinkering with iMovie and Final Cut Pro was a turning point in the semester. Students had three weeks to tinker and complete a two- to three-minute digital story on a personal topic of their choice. One class session was devoted to visiting the university's Creative Lab for group and one-on-one tutorials. Several students on their own also accessed video tutorials on YouTube; two students went as far as visiting an Apple store for additional one-on-one tutorials on iMovie (at no cost). Another class session was spent viewing a preliminary version of the digital stories in small groups for feedback.

The subsequent class session was the digital story videocast; this involved uploading the videos to our YouTube channel, an in-house screening, and a collective feedback forum after the screening. The latter surprisingly ended with what seemed an on-the-spot jury selection of three digital stories based on quality. That is, the class asked to view three specific digital stories for a second time to discuss unique or standout technical aspects of the production. I followed up with each of the students to conduct a producer's commentary as a way to learn more about their digital stories. This entailed having a producer watch the digital story and simultaneously make comments during playback; one producer's commentary is provided below. Given the personal nature of the digital stories (all but one revealed the student's likeness as well as friends and family members), we as a class decided to keep the YouTube channel private to accommodate concerns about privacy (a topic we had discussed earlier in the semester).

For me, the exercise of tinkering with media production was an important part of the learning process.[3] My hope in tasking students with a digital story was that it would expand their understanding of genres of participation while preparing them for the next and final project. As we shall see, the digital story project served as a stepping stone toward a more elaborate media-making endeavor intersecting with participatory politics because of the deliberate creation of alternative and activist new media.

Digital Story: Reflection and Producer's Commentary

A sophomore White male student named Alvin produced a digital story titled "When I Travel." [4] Alvin had not declared a major but he mentioned having strong interests in music and the visual arts. He was interested in the theory and application of new media literacies but had minimal experience in media production. Alvin wrote "When I Travel" to serve as the script for the voice-narration of the digital story with a total running time of 2:19 minutes. Figure 5 details the key elements of the digital story. The video consisted of nineteen photographs taken by Alvin himself. Alvin recorded at home the somber sound of instrumental piano playing along the narration in the background.

To help students make sense of their own experience working with new media literacies, I had asked all students to write a two- to three-page reflection paper. This was done prior to asking several students for a producer's commentary. I provided sample reflection questions such as, *What was the production process like for you? What tools did you choose and why? How much time did the production take? Were there any challenges? What did you learn in creating the digital story?* The reflection was an opportunity for students to assess their own work and also to gauge their own learning in the class. As an instructor, I drew on reflection papers to better understand the digital stories. In his paper, Alvin wrote:

> The choosing and ordering of my photography was distinctly difficult. . . in pursuit of photographs of both high visual quality and high communicative quality (I wanted the chosen photographs to be able to tell their own story / to be able to speak for themselves). . . . Overall, the process was of moderate difficulty (in terms of school

NARRATION/POEM	TIME	VISUAL/SIGN	EFFECTS
	0:00	{piano starts}	Fade in
When I travel	0:04	title	Black
I find color	0:09	1 cat	Cross-dissolve
In colorful cities	0:17	2 San Francisco	Cross-dissolve
In colorful bases	0:22	3 shipyard	Cross-dissolve
I find people	0:29	4 man	Cross-dissolve
And faces	0:35	5 man 6 man w/ hat	Cross-dissolve
Their smiles	0:46	7 woman	Cross-dissolve
Their friendships	0:53	8 two men 9 pedestrians	Cross-dissolve
When I travel	1:05	10 "got gas" sign	Cross-dissolve
I find landscapes	1:06		Cross-dissolve
And streets	1:12	11 street on hill	Cross-dissolve
And fog	1:18	12 fog 13 street with cars	Cross-dissolve
I find new friends	1:28	14 dog 15 bird	Cross-dissolve
And old places	1:41	16 trees 17 meadow	Cross-dissolve
Most importantly	1:54	18 moss	Cross-dissolve
I find myself	2:00	19 reflection	Cross-dissolve
	2:06		Fade to black
	2:09	credits	Fade out
	2:14	{piano ends}	Black

FIGURE 5. Alvin's "When I Travel." Portraits of individuals not included.

assignments I have had to do in the past). The most difficult part was, by far, choosing what issue/theme to talk about . . . it is not an easy task to choose something (whether it be words, music, photography, or video) to represent oneself. I evaded this task, in part, by *showing things I created rather than things of me* (photographs/ videos/stories of me). This is, perhaps, what is communicated to the audience at the end of the day; I express myself best by producing rather than attempting autobiography or auto-photography. This is something I may not have realized during the process but in having reflected, I realize it now. [emphasis added]

In his reflection, Alvin disclosed that despite the moderate difficulty he chose to focus on the communicative logic of the visuals and the assemblage of his own photographs to tell a story. Alvin used multiple modes such as the poem as narration, photographs as visuals, and instrumental piano as background music to pull together segments of his travels to northern California and the Northwest. Writing the reflection allowed Alvin to realize the reasons for his choices. From this reflection, the importance of tinkering with digital tools in working with new media literacies is affirmed. As well, the notion of assemblage or the gathering of prefabricated materials to represent oneself as discussed in chapter 1 surfaces as integral to the production process.

Alvin's producer's commentary, which came after the reflection paper, offered another dimension of analysis centered on the producer's stylistic choices. The commentary provided a perspective on intertextuality, multimodality, and symbolic creativity embedded in the digital story video with insights into Alvin's DIY production process, image by image. Understanding the media production process with such insights allowed me as a facilitator of learning to shape the direction of the NML class toward the final project. Alvin shared that each image included in the digital story was taken with his digital single-lens reflex camera. He also pointed out that to him his camera was a tool for seeing the world. This observation prompted me to engage students in a discussion during class about using their eye as a way to see and interpret the world around them. I encouraged students to apply this interpretive lens whenever they snapped photos or captured video footage for their social action projects.

Different from a reflection paper, Alvin's producer's commentary offered a deeper view of what was involved behind the scenes of the digital story. Alvin watched and discussed what appeared on the screen *in real time,* noting details about the who, what, where, when, and why to further clarify his choices. Below is an excerpt from the commentary:

0:00   This is the title shot.
There's a cat that I met in Oakland, California.
And this is San Francisco, um, from a hill.

This is kind of chronological.

And this is Seattle, um.

0:30   Yeah, there's a guy I met who was asking why I was, like, taking pictures of old buildings so I took a picture of him instead. And asked to take this guy's picture as well . . .

Using an iMac computer to play back the video while recording his producer's commentary, Alvin pointed out the stylistic choices (e.g., photographs, sound of piano for mood) and various techniques (e.g., transition effects) from his point of view as photographer/producer/ storyteller. Alvin explained all nineteen images in detail and in doing so made apparent the dynamic nature of the interactions he had with people, things, and places during his travels. For example, the cat in Oakland or the guy in San Francisco, even old buildings and the larger environment, influenced the range of photographic subjects to which Alvin had access. Such interactions allowed for prefabricated materials and fragments in art-making that he later reassembled to create the digital story. Retelling his production process in this fashion also situated Alvin in the context of the social and cultural experiences he represents in the digital story.

The commentary articulates the rhizomatic influences in art-making and provides greater insight for understanding his stylistic choices (Deleuze and Guattari 1987; Hodge and Kress 1988). What emerged in commentating on the digital story is the significance of assemblage in media production that renders the construction of meaning connectable and modifiable across time, space, and matter. Toward the end of the playback session of the commentary, Alvin added:

> Things sort of *fell into place in a way that I wouldn't have expected them to*, like, as I already said, with the music and the transitions. I sort of planned it but it also just sort of, like, happened to work. Um yeah . . . I gave myself, like, a limited amount of time to do it which I think is a good thing because then, like, I didn't procrastinate. . . . I guess that pressure plus having the right software and the right, like, archive of stuff, it made it kind of easy, I guess. [emphasis added]

Through the producer's commentary, it became apparent how the element of uncertainty in media production serves student learning. It affirmed that learning is about trying something new, tinkering with technology, and drawing on assemblage in digital storytelling. The latter, as Alvin pointed out, may or may not yield what the producer expects the final outcome of media production to be. Yet there is learning embedded in the doing. As illustrated in the example, the producer's commentary provided Alvin an opportunity to acknowledge not only his own stylistic choices but also the sometimes implicit learning that happens through the enactment of new media literacies in digital storytelling. Things fall into place because a producer has directed things into place. That form of agency in learning deserves recognition, especially in today's technology-rich learning environments where students are experimenting with different tools for different purposes in their lives.

Digital storytelling is now an integral part of many classrooms. It has theoretical and practical implications relevant to how students draw on their experiences and tell stories that matter to them, how stories come together as assemblage, and what can happen in the process of media production to further inform teaching and learning with technology. Having students create producer's commentary as a method for a deeper analysis of their work offered more explicit understandings of the production and learning process, the states or recombinant layers of meaning within the digital story from the student's perspective, and elements behind the scenes that otherwise might not have been captured through traditional methods such as reflection papers or class memos. Specific to teaching and teacher education (Matias and Grosland 2016; Robin 2008), digital storytelling has been key to inform practice and support teacher development in revelatory ways.

Shifting to Alternative and Activist New Media

With the deployment of new media literacies as a concept and subsequent course-related activities, it became clear that the students and I were enacting various theories into practice. Blogging, group presentations, the experiential learning poster project, and the digital story all seemed essential but still incomplete pedagogically. The idea of wielding voice and influence on issues of public concern as participatory politics was catalytic. Around week nine, we proceeded to draw on what Lievrouw calls alternative and activist new media as a way to push our thinking toward the transformative potential of new media literacies.

According to Lievrouw, alternative and activist new media "employ or modify the communication artifacts, practices, and social arrangements of new and information and communication technologies to challenge or alter dominant, expected, or accepted ways of doing society, culture, and politics" (2011, 19). Genres of alternative and activist new media include culture jamming, participatory journalism, alternative computing, mediated mobilization, and commons knowledge. Attentive to changing practices, Lievrouw argues that at the heart of such new social strategies are mediations, or the continuous and mutual reshaping of the "relationship between people's uses of technology and their communicative action that produces social and technological change" (231). While reading Lievrouw's work, we also derived perspectives from Yang (2007) on youth walkouts and Cohen et al. (2012) on youth participatory politics. It was valuable to see examples of young people engaging in the pleasure and politics of everyday life, including school, and using technology to participate online through mediated expressions. This was significant for us in the process of expanding the notion of participatory politics as voluntary acts converging in institutional spaces. The link between theory and practice through the lens of alternative and activist new media led us to explicit connections between what we had done so far and the looming social action project. We recognized that our own class blog served as an example of participatory journalism and commons knowledge. As well, we claimed the digital stories and group presentations as participatory, mediated expressions that circulated information among us (regardless of group size). We were, in essence, producing knowledge with new media literacies at play. My point here (and in the analysis of the social action project below) is that pedagogy was integral to the thinking, theory building, and exchange.

My Role as Teacher and Learner

It is important to share my positioning in relation to pedagogical strategies. In this new media literacies class, I was an active participant who helped shape the material, spatial, and discursive aspects of the course. I collected student work produced during the semester, including print and digital materials. The aforementioned activities and assignments yielded the following: 9 visual prompts on the class blog with a total of 64 comments; 7 group presentations with either PowerPoint or Prezi slides; 8 group analyses and posters on technology-rich environments; 13 personal digital stories; and 6 social action video documentaries with accompanying interactive websites. To gain some sense of participants as individuals and as a group, I asked students on the first day of class to fill out an information sheet with general questions about their personal background, academic and social interests, media production experience, and reasons for taking the course. I archived the information sheet (see Appendix C for a summary of what students shared).[5]

As mentioned, the new media literacies course was open to undergraduate and graduate students. Students' ages ranged from 19 to 25 with the exception of one, a 33-year-old middle school teacher whose eight years of teaching experience were invaluable in our discussions about current practices of new media literacies in schools. Seven students had explicit interests in education or had been working in educational settings through after-school programs. Later in the semester, I administered a self-evaluation (or what I refer to as "check-in") in week eight and another ("check-out") in week fifteen (separate from the university course evaluations). The check-in centered on students' progress in the course and the check-out served as an overall self-assessment with space to indicate any "take-aways" about new media literacies. For both the digital story and social action project, an informal reflection on the media-making process was submitted as part of the assignment. Additionally, I wrote memos about each class session.

As an instructor wearing both researcher and participant hats, I needed to be transparent about the aims of the course and the particular ways in which I was deploying "new media literacies" through specific activities. On the first day of class, I described the nature of the course and informed students that I was also conducting a teacher inquiry with an emphasis on pedagogy. I underscored that their enrollment in the course implied that they were giving informal consent.[6] About one-third of the students did not show up beyond the first week of classes. During the weeks leading up to week ten, the set of readings and assignments knowingly *and* unknowingly shaped the learning process toward alternative and activist new media. An "ethos" of collaboration, participation, and distributed expertise seemed to be evolving from theory building to grounded practice (Lankshear and Knobel 2006).

The culmination of the class was to be a public screening of students' work, held at a nearby museum. Based on my observations, students were keen on the event, debating about methods of attracting a broad audience. Initial conversations about location and venue, accessibility (free admission and transportation), date, time of day, event title, and types of publicity shaped the pre-planning. While we preferred an evening on the last week of classes, the museum's schedule only allowed for a weekend event. We agreed to hold the public screening on a Saturday afternoon during a time when, we were told, visitors across age groups flock to the museum; the venue we selected inside was the Grand Hall, where the most traffic occurs. We envisioned a large viewing screen and the voices within each video filling up the space; we also envisioned easels on the periphery for sharing the technology-rich environment posters so that these would become part of the museum's exhibit, at least for that time period. With these ideas and plans, I communicated with the museum's staff to coordinate the event.

By week ten, primed for a public screening of their work, students submitted final project proposals along with a project timeline. We spent the majority of that class session discussing different possibilities for moving forward and how to responsibly approach the social and educational issues they had identified (see Figure 6). We eventually merged overlapping interests and topics to create five groups of two and one group of three students. To guide students in their inquiry, I specifically asked questions about ontology and epistemology in relation to knowledge production (i.e., what it means to examine social or cultural phenomena, how one can be positioned or privileged in particular environments, how one's view of the world informs ways of knowing or doing, etc.). It was important to connect what we were doing to what Kellner and Share (2007) describe as the work of critical media literacies. Drawing from class notes and a memo from that day, I shared the following with students: "Things do not just appear as they are; things are constructed and represented using language and other tools in particular ways for various purposes, including new media; those constructions and representations have different implications for different people."

Guiding the Process

With this premise in mind, I proceeded to urge students to think about settings, participants, access, ethics, and representation with respect to each of their projects. For example, I posed questions such as Who will help inform your topic of choice? How will you gain access to potential participants? What types of questions will you ask interviewees? In what ways will the social action project you plan to pursue provide an "alternative" view of the topic? How do you know it's "alternative"? The latter questions proved difficult to answer because students depended largely on what the inquiry would yield. With some contemplation of the serious yet uncertain nature of inquiry, students went on to ask their own questions and seek the support of the larger community in the process of trying to find answers.

The inquiry that unfolded was paired with readings on critical media pedagogy (Morrell et al. 2013), popular culture and teaching in urban schools (Mahiri 2006; Philip and Garcia 2013), remix and youth media (Jocson 2013a; Soep 2011; Vasudevan 2010), and copyright and fair use in education (Hobbs and Donnelly 2011), to name a few.[7] Doing the work in/with new media literacies as advocates was in part about reflecting on our own sense of social justice using arts-based work, while also sorting out our own practices within digital media culture (Kuttner 2015; Mihailidis 2014). Engaging in the politics of knowledge production proved to be a fruitful exercise for seeing one's self as a member of a larger cultural milieu and for reflecting on how that cultural milieu is ever-changing, with mediation between the human, the material, the discursive, and the digital. The social action project was upon us.

Social Action Projects

Students in the NML class were not new to conducting inquiry. They were part of a university that prides itself on being a research institution. However, as revealed in the project proposals and reflection papers, this type of inquiry, where students are positioned as questioning normalized discourses and using new media tools to inquire and disseminate findings (versus a written report, thesis paper, or poster presentation) had been rare. Doing critical inquiry that involved input from the larger community to promote social awareness and civic dialogue was even more rare. Having some sense of the liminal space we inhabited at the university, I discussed in class the core values guiding our work, that we were drawing on a model of connected learning concerned with equity, full participation, and social connection (Ito et al. 2013; Ito et al.

2015). By week eleven, students had identified participants and churned out questions for use in their interviews. I reminded the class to obtain written permission to interview or record participants agreeing to have their likeness appear on video. For those conducting inquiry in schools, I emphasized the ethics involved in working with minors. I distributed a template for obtaining parental consent for minors, as several students had planned on interviewing high school aged youth to inform their project. There were no risks or benefits to participants, and the social action project was intended for educational purposes only.

Through dialogue and collective feedback during week eleven's class session, it became apparent to me that the social and/or educational issues selected by the students were building on concurrent courses, working theses, or preliminary research in their academic trajectory. The selection of a social or educational issue, then, was not random or arbitrary, which sometimes happens when the learning objective turns into appeasing the instructor or fulfilling a course requirement; rather, the selection was purposefully connected and contingent upon other discourses in which students had participated. Additionally, the selection of group partners was also purposeful to complement students' interests.

By week twelve, I had become more attentive to the emerging ethos that was developing through *collaboration* with peers and community members, *participation* in interest-driven inquiry centered on social or educational issues, and *distributed expertise* in the learning process that ultimately led to video documentaries and interactive websites. At this stage, most of the students' planned interviews had been completed and researching the topic online or reviewing literature began. Students in their respective groups had tasked themselves with different respon-sibilities, and by week thirteen, several groups had begun pulling to-gether video footage and other visual materials to create an edited time-line using iMovie or Final Cut Pro. We discussed in class the difficulty of cutting down footage to fit into a five to eight minute narrative. We consulted each other for collective feedback. By week fourteen, students had produced a rough cut of the video documentary and a preliminary interactive website. Once again, we consulted each other for collective feedback; this was a key moment, as students had less than a week to make revisions and complete the video documentary for the public screening. The anxious countdown to the public screening was evident as students worked around the clock until the evening before the event. With the submitted video documentaries, I created a DVD containing all six projects to use for playback at the public screening the next day.

Analyzing What and How Students Produced

A content multimodal analysis of the social action video documentaries shows the interweaving of voice-narration, written text, visual text, and sound/instrumental track. Figure 6 provides details on each video docu-

GROUP #	TITLE	TOPIC	LENGTH
1	"The District: A Unique Perspective" (by Anna and Devon)	Loss of accreditation, examining the issue with voices of students	6:09
2	"The Divide" (by Amy and Janet)	Segregation by race and class, questioning the dividing line	6:02
3	"Social Change" (by Alvin and Eddie)	Community needs, exploring and representing community ideas	5:24
4	"Innovative" (by Amber, Heather, and Jim)	School to prison pipeline, interrupting through education	5:33
5	"The Politics of Change" (by Kelly and Samantha)	Homelessness, acknowledging lack of awareness and disconnect between university and community	8:15
6	"We're All Born Artists" (by Danny and Val)	Arts education, challenging cutbacks to support the development of creative capacities of children	7:45

FIGURE 6. *Social Action Projects: Video Documentaries. Titles slightly modified for purposes of anonymity.*

mentary. In previous studies, I used a matrix for analyzing multimedia texts with attention to the script, image, and sound of multimedia texts, and the various aesthetic, conceptual, and technical elements involved in media production (see Appendix A). Here, the interweaving of voice-narration, written text, visual text, and sound/instrumental track reflects the multiple layers constituting each video documentary. The inquiry part of the project yielded video interviews and original footage of the local setting as well as appropriated video and still images that were (re)assembled using an editing tool to frame the select topic.

GROUP #	CONTENT	NUMBER OF VIDEO INTERVIEWS AND ORIGINAL FOOTAGE	NUMBER OF APPROPRIATED VIDEO FOOTAGE AND STILL IMAGES
1	Voiceover-narration (single) Written text Visual text Sound/instrumental	3 video interviews (3 community members: high-school youth)	4 videos 13 still images
2	Voiceover-narration (double) Written text Visual text Sound/instrumental	1 original footage 5 video interviews (4 community members; 1 university student)	2 videos 1 still image
3	Voiceover-narration (double) Written text Visual text Sound/instrumental	12 video interviews (9 community members; 1 university student; 2 university students: creators)	8 still images
4	Voiceover-narration (single) Written text Visual text Sound/instrumental	1 video interview (1 university faculty)	3 videos 11 still images
5	Voiceover-narration (single) Written text Visual text	10 video interviews (7 university students; 1 university faculty; 2 community members)	
6	Voiceover-narration (double) Written text Visual text Sound/instrumental track	2 video interviews (1 teacher; 1 student)	5 videos 20 still images

The ethos of collaboration, participation, and distributed expertise that had been a part of our learning process surfaced in support of the social action projects. As revealed in student reflection papers, *collaboration* with peers and community members, *participation* in interest-driven inquiry, and *distributed expertise* through the production of video documentaries and interactive websites (along with a public screening) helped to realize the transformative potential of new media literacies as social action. From inquiry to media production, the learning process centered on shared purpose, hands-on production, and open networks.[8] According to students, it was important to build on each other's strengths, to be diligent about exploring the select topic, and to apply their knowledge from tinkering with digital media technologies to creating and disseminating "alternative" texts. For example, Val of group 6 pointed out the following in his reflection paper:

> We were able to handle technical aspects of the project simultaneously, employing new media literacy in sharing a Google document on which we proposed ideas and drafted a script. We maintained a healthy amount of trust between the division of responsibilities, and were able to meet regularly to flesh out the final product. Because [Danny] had access to teachers and students at [school], he was able to interview/survey individuals, and we incorporated that content into our project. I found myself handling the script-writing, which required balancing a well-framed argument with an engaging narrative arc. We both accessed footage through YouTube to serve as additional support for our message of the importance of arts education in public schools.

Danny shared a similar appreciation for their work on the project and indicated the extent of engaging participatory politics through video production and website creation to circulate among a larger audience. In his reflection paper, he wrote:

> [Val] and I met on several occasions, breaking the project up into smaller chunks so that we could work on multiple aspects simultaneously.... Knowing several art teachers, and having direct contact with students each day, I chose to help complete [the interview] section. I used a digital camcorder to interview [a teacher] and

chose to create a brief questionnaire for the students. . . The last component was the website. On the "About" tab we wrote a quick summary outlining the problem of the arts declining within public schools. I gave each of my students a four-question survey asking them why the arts in school are important. We selected several answers to include on the "Student Voice" section [of the website]. We also created a "Resource" tab where we linked up many of the resources we found for our project and a couple of arts programs [in the local area]. Last we embedded our iMovie within the website.

In another example, Kelly of group 5 noted the necessity of working collaboratively yet marked challenges along the way:

> We tried to do it all together. Of course, there were scheduling issues or technology issues. . . [for example] extenuating circumstances like how all of our footage was on one computer, making it hard to work simultaneously and productively. . . . We interviewed several students, one faculty, and two homeless participants. We had all this footage but it was hard to figure out what to include.

Samantha echoed similar sentiments about collaboration and distributed expertise. Noteworthy in her reflection paper is a critical recognition of media making and community building as participatory politics:

> We took advantage of one another's strengths. [Kelly] is in Communication Design and is artistically inclined. All of the drawings and doodles that you find in our movie are her creations. I am a seasoned public speaker, so it's my voice you hear in the narration. Overall, the documentary came out of a strong sense of urgency regarding the issue of connecting our [university] peers to our greater [local/city] surroundings. We wanted to shine light on the fact that our school exists in a much bigger community with different kinds of people, many of whom come from privileged backgrounds. So did we.

Upon a closer look at the student reflections along with the video documentaries, I noticed that two groups (#1, #3) exercised division of labor in order to complete the project in a timely manner, while four groups (#2, #4, #5, #6) jointly conducted different aspects of the project such as interviewing participants, writing a script, editing the video, and later creating an interactive website. Additionally, I noticed the deployment of new media literacies to be pragmatic in order to complete different tasks. These new media literacies became evident: tinkering or experimenting with digital media technologies (*play*); adopting roles or performing identities to conduct interviews with different people inside and outside the university context (*performance*); sampling and remixing media content (*appropriation*); shifting focus while tending to multiple commitments as students (*multitasking*); expanding one's mental capacities through new tools and new experiences (*distributed cognition*); pooling knowledge and sharing notes toward a particular purpose (*collective intelligence*); evaluating the reliability and credibility of information sources (*judgment*); following the flow of stories and information across multiple media (*transmedia navigation*); collecting and circulating information to others (*networking*); traveling across different communities and respecting multiple perspectives (*negotiation*); and translating information into visual models as a form of communication (*visualization*).

Such new media literacies were central in the completion of the social action projects; they were key practices in the planning, design, implementation, and dissemination. The social action projects created opportunities for "doing" participatory politics—from brainstorming topics to researching online, interviewing local participants in context, editing original and found footage to produce a video, building an interactive website, and sharing the combined material with a public audience. The "doing" was akin to what Ratto and Boler (2014) have termed "DIY citizenship"; that is, students assumed active roles as tinkerers and media makers in the process. Within the learning and production process were also opportunities for self-reflection. Thus, the pursuit of "alternative" media making was, in turn, a pursuit of shifting views about ourselves as participants in the research and as members of society with the ability to produce knowledge, to use particular forms of knowledge to challenge normalized ways of thinking and doing, and to be open to and informed by multiple ways of knowing in recognition of possible entangled lives and experiences (Deleuze and Guattari 1987). New media literacies as social action pedagogically oriented us to engage in the politics of knowledge production.

The Politics of Knowledge Production

Evident in the reflection papers and my observations of class sessions were insights gained from doing critical inquiry. The inductive approach was helpful for students to recognize the limitations as well as tensions that emerged through collaboration with peers and community members. In a group share-out during class, one group (#2) pointed out the difficulty of having differing views on information gathering, who they should interview and where, who should conduct the interview based on social perceptions about race and gender, and to what extent their identity markers and rapport within the local community can shape how interview participants respond to them and their questions. Two groups (#1, #4) revealed the limited or narrow perspective represented in their videos due to the low number of participants and interviews in the inquiry process. In contrast, three groups (#3, #5, #6) noted having more than enough interviews and footage from which to select for inclusion in the video; that is, they had far more available footage to whittle down during editing. Three groups (#1, #4, #5) whose topics involved either minors or vulnerable populations also expressed ethical considerations that limited their access to participants or their ability to record using a video camera.

In hindsight, these revelations about the nature of inquiry affirmed that knowledge is constructed and that the subjective representations of any experience through the exchange of meanings always remains incomplete (Denzin 2014; Hall 1997). Processes of cultural production always omit someone or something. Despite efforts toward alternative and activist new media, the mediation between the human, the material, the discursive, and the digital in the social action projects illustrates the value of learning with/from each other and across multiple perspectives in an ever-changing cultural milieu. The social action projects did not end when the video documentaries were screened at the museum. Soon after, the interactive websites were released to promote continued dialogue. At the initial writing of this narrative, each respective website had accumulated traffic and comments from a number of visitors. Both the community sharing and the distribution of videos rendered a kind of participatory politics that was enabled by a course theorizing on new media literacies.

Finally, as expressed on the last day of class, all students in the course recounted theory building and grounded practice as helpful to seeing themselves differently in a digitally mediated world. In particular, the tinkering with digital media technologies through purposeful assignments expanded their media production experience and furthered their thinking about what it meant to consume, produce, and share media content in the realm of DIY citizenship. The following excerpts from the end of the semester check-out highlight students' take-aways:

> I now understand more concretely the importance of new media literacy . . . to strive to make education a means of improving the world around us.

> I learned that new media literacy is a living entity. It is constantly growing and changing as we evolve as a people. Utilizing these tools will always be a constant battle in my classroom.

> I genuinely enjoyed completing the assignments because they've challenged me to try new things and develop new skills and engage with new and different kinds of people.

> I think this class made me more aware. . . . I loved the incorporation of the [larger] community, something so important yet not focused on here at [the university] enough.

Noteworthy in the responses are the conceptualization and application of new media literacies that had guided the course. Appendix C shows all of the student responses paired with reasons for taking the course. Comparing various sets of responses allowed me to realize what had taken place throughout the semester in relation to learning and change. The course had ended yet I was left wondering about pedagogical possibilities.

Reflexive Teaching and Learning

In this new media literacies course, I was privileged to work with students who were willing to go with me pedagogically. I was also privileged to have had university resources to help accommodate our needs, including a classroom inside the main campus library that enabled collaborative learning and a Creative Lab with digital media technologies that provided students with equipment and tutorials. I remain grateful for the opportunity to have facilitated (and participated in) a kind of learning with the support of the larger community. The lessons are many. This narrative is an attempt to share some insights into new media literacies, youth cultural production, and participatory politics. Reflexively, it is important to note the limitations in my own inquiry. These include the small number of students enrolled in the course as represented here, the university context in which the course was offered, the specific readings and assignments that guided the course, and the particularities of our experience subject to a specific space and time in the urban Midwest. To protect the identities of students and community members, the links to the video documentaries and interactive websites are not included in this writing. Sharing specific aspects of the learning process has been my task in order to point out pedagogical possibilities.

The implications of new media literacies extend beyond research. As a teacher, I continue to grapple with lessons learned about theory building and classroom practice. What does it mean to draw on new media literacies as a way to understand the politics of knowledge production with DIY tools more readily available now than ever before? In what ways does an ethos of collaboration, participation, and distributed expertise bust the very bubble that we as learners, creators, and tinkerers operate within, and in what ways does it allow us to become more thoughtful in the process of becoming the learners, creators, and tinkerers we have yet to be? How should curriculum be shaped with digital media, democracy, and justice at the center of pedagogy?

From this particular new media literacies course, it became apparent that continued work is necessary to understand the blurring lines of youth cultural production and participatory politics. For example, I wonder what would have happened if students and I had an opportunity to revisit the interactive websites, to ask each other questions about meaning and representation, or to repurpose the written and visual texts gathered by students toward the further remaking of the material, the discursive, and the digital? What knowledges and positionings would future opportunities for critical making yield? What new DIY tools would allow for different kinds of youth cultural production and participatory politics in the classroom? Whose voices would be included, and from whose perspectives? These questions point back to the theorizing of new media literacies that had taken place and the practices that had emerged along the way to further explore the politics of knowledge production.

Now What?

New media literacies as a topic and an area of study are still evolving. In this chapter, it has been important to identify the ways in which university students leveraged new media literacies to engage in theory building and grounded practice. I draw on what happened in my own class to discuss specific aspects of the teaching, learning, and production process, an opportunity to see that what we were doing in the course had social consequences. The work produced through course assignments and activities demonstrate that youth cultural production and participatory politics were shaped by our social and cultural experiences. In part, alternative and activist media practices allowed for an exploration of voice and influence on issues of public concern (Cohen et al. 2012). New media literacies as social action emerged as a key insight pointing to youth media as pedagogy. What became evident in the teaching, learning, and production process were lessons about how mediation between the human, the material, the discursive, and the digital can offer new experiences and new possibilities.

There is room to grow and to (re)imagine critical making differently. An ethos of collaboration, participation, and distributed expertise may have been fleeting in the context of a semester-long course. My hope is that, while school, work, or life unfolds in each of their respective contexts, students continue to leverage new media literacies in ways that question or challenge normative discourses. This hope represents a shift toward seeking alternative possibilities, perhaps a (re)interpretation, a (re)representation, or a (re)construction of lived and constructed realities. The uncertainty of becoming active citizens with the use of digital media technologies and shifting everyday practice was (and is still) part of the journey. Next, the final chapter pulls together ideas presented in this book to suggest assemblage, critical solidarity, place-making, and pedagogy as key to understanding youth media in participatory cultures.

Translocal Possibilities and the Politics of Media Making

"Have you seen the video? Have you seen it?" I blurted out from across the lobby of the Lake Arrowhead Conference Center. "It's been blowing up on social media!" Before I could say anything else, Tyrone Howard smiled and said, "Yes, that was done by one of my students." I chuckled, having forgotten how small the world is. The video had just reached my Facebook page a few minutes earlier and I thought I was actually sharing news with him. Tyrone is a professor of education at UCLA and teaches courses on race and class as well as the sociology of education; he also directs the UCLA Black Male Institute. The lobby thinned out quickly as guests and attendees proceeded to the second-floor lecture hall. It was minutes before Tyrone's keynote presentation for the annual fall conference of the University of California All Campus Consortium on Research for Diversity (UC ACCORD). There we all were in the mountains of the San Bernardino National Forest. At the reception immediately after his talk, Tyrone and I had an opportunity to revisit the trending video that since then has been key to my teaching and thinking around media production. The video is a multimedia poem created by Sy Stokes. As a former UC ACCORD fellow, I was invited back to the conference that year, coincidentally, to be a featured speaker on the topic of poetry and transformative education.

This chapter returns to the notion of assemblage described in chapter 1. This time, I extend the theorizing to be more inclusive of translocal practices that were central to youth media as critical solidarity in chapter 2, as place-making in chapter 3, and as pedagogy in chapter 4. It is important to point out that translocalism is further amplified by today's technologies and participatory cultures. The translocal nature of the media produced by young people, often with a call to disrupt power structures embedded in the message, is worthy of attention. It is here that I join the conversation to offer a pedagogical perspective on translocal assemblage. In what ways can translocal assemblage through media making shape discourses of power? In what ways do youth-produced videos resonate across locales to address or call out educational and social inequities toward disrupting power structures? I share some insights to highlight the ways in which cultural material can travel to incite the exchange of ideas toward the creation of alternative media. That youth are enacting their self-interests and finding civic resources to do so is key in the discussion. Translocal assemblages framed within the blurred lines of youth cultural production and participatory politics are important for advancing critical education. (To reiterate, the term "youth" as used in this book refers to those ages 15–24 to include students' experiences during their time in college.)

The explosion of digital media technology in youth's lives has propelled research agendas in digital media and learning in order to understand media ecologies, networked publics, and peer-based genres of participation among youth (boyd 2014; Ito 2010). Projects like YOUmedia inside Chicago's Harold Washington public library have explored the different ways that youth participate in interest- or friendship-driven activities through a digital youth network (Pinkard and Austin 2011). Linking youth's engagement with digital media technology marks current directions in connected learning to build learning environments that support models of learning oriented toward educational equity (Ito et al. 2013). This approach to connected learning suggests possibilities for innovative practice in education. One such possibility, as discussed in previous chapters, is through DIY to DIT production and distribution to wide audiences, and what happens when youth connect and build on each other's work to assert themselves in the new media landscape.

Participatory Politics and the Translocal

Currently, there is a growing cultural and social movement among youth who draw on spoken word poetry and media production as they participate in the new media landscape. Multimedia poems have appeared on social media sites such as YouTube and Vimeo as a form of participatory politics. According to Cohen et al. (2012), participatory politics are interactive, peer-based acts that have the ability to reach large audiences, shape agendas through dialogue, and exert greater agency through the circulation of information and the production of original content, both online and offline. As noted in the previous chapter, the notion of participatory politics is seen as wielding voice and influence on issues of public concern without being guided by deference to elites or formal institutions. The idea of participatory politics provides a way of understanding the range of activities that support young people's agency in public spheres (Soep 2014). For example, young people are experimenting with bottom-up tactics to challenge the social order. Tactics of participatory politics include mobilizing civic capacity within networks, creating content worlds, finding and sharing information through public data archives, designing tools and platforms to advance the public good, and at times covering tracks and protecting information from discovery. These tactics require particular kinds of practices in learning environments that spark curiosity and action.

In my work with secondary and college-level students, I have been privileged to design learning environments that blur the lines of youth cultural production and participatory politics. I have been attentive to how participatory politics are pedagogically operational in critical education despite the constraints of the classroom (Anyon 2009a). What I have found in youth media production as part of a growing participatory culture are idiosyncratic uptakes where remix and the combined talents of youth writers/performers and media producers establish a critical solidarity, a social commitment to alliance that may include responses to media representations or a shared critique (Ferguson 2001). Chapter 2 provided examples of critical solidarity across genre practices of spoken word poetry and filmmaking, respectively. In this chapter, I pick up the discussion and revisit the notion of remix to frame translocal practices, or what McFarlane (2009) calls "translocal assemblage," wherein individuals and groups engage in the exchange of ideas across space and time.

I highlight one multimedia poem produced by a group of racialized minority students at one American university. Soon after, the multimedia poem was remixed into another multimedia poem by another group of students at a different university to demonstrate the potential of translocal assemblage and the practice of alternative media in the movement toward racial justice (note: viewing the videos beforehand may be helpful to grasp the extent of the analysis presented here).[1] Both multimedia poems focused on the underrepresentation of students of color, particularly from the perspective of African American and Black male students at their respective universities. Together, they exemplify the affordances of networked publics (persistence, visibility, spreadability, and searchability) that enabled interactions between different sets of students over time and context (boyd 2014). The multimedia poems also display students connecting to build on each other's work as a form of participatory politics.

With the fluidity of translocal assemblage, I drew on these multimedia poems to engage my own students in DIY and DIT productions of alternative media in the college classroom. The course through which this production took place provided opportunities for translocal practices to be linked to the study of new media literacies (see chapter 4). In seeking ways to understand youth media as a site for innovative teaching and learning in the college classroom, I began examining local and translocal practices of youth in high school classrooms and other educational settings, especially at the intersection of literary and media arts. This approach was influential for understanding how some youth construct versions of self or represent their social worlds through poems, digital stories, short documentaries, and experimental videos. Such genres of media production fall within what Lievrouw (2011) describes as alternative and activist new media that blur the lines between culture jamming (cultural critique), participatory journalism (covering underreported groups and issues), and commons knowledge (mobilizing "outsider" knowledge). That students are the center of blurring these lines is noteworthy. Thus, as a departure point for understanding translocal practices via multimedia poems, I built on existing literature that treats poetry as a form of cultural politics grounded in the Black Arts Movement.

As Fisher points out, it is important to recognize the historical continuum of Black literate traditions that were linked to Black people's struggle to pursue freedom, literacy, and education. Such efforts remain key for encouraging poets and writers (youth and adults alike) to become "educators, activists, community organizers, and leaders" in (re)defining Black literate lives (2009, 3). In the classroom and after-school programs, poetry has served as a pedagogical tool for engaging students in forms of writing and spoken word performance to make sense of their realities in connection to literacy and social justice (Fisher 2007; Jocson 2008; Stovall 2006a). Emerging from this growing cultural practice across social groups domestically and internationally are what Ingalis (2012) calls "poet-citizens," those who use poetry as a rhetorical conduit to inspire civic engagement.

The poets and producers featured in this chapter exhibit some possibilities of poetry as a form of cultural politics combined with youth media making. Through decades of cultural movements, poetry has (re)emerged arguably more visible than ever through social media and advances in technology. Youth are marking their place in history through multimedia poems and bespeaking a politics of difference toward a cultural-political project. Media production in this light provides a new way of writing a politicized/ing self. Multimedia poems taking the form of videos become a call for recognition aimed to disrupt power. As cultural material, the multimedia poems also become a catalyst for blurring and enabling other genres of alternative media, as was the case in my class. Without shying away from concerns over race relations and racial justice, it is worthwhile to understand the social consequence of media production, particularly when educational and social policies have diminished in an era of alienation and the disposability of youth (Giroux 2012).

Youth engaging in writing and spoken word poetry have pushed me to explore the "translocal" in youth cultural production and participatory politics. A focus on the "translocal" makes explicit the sometimes subtle nature of cultural flows in the movement of ideas and practices across space and time. Translocal assemblage, as illustrated in the discussion, is important for understanding the relational impact of new technologies on teaching and learning that have direct consequences for critical education. Translocal assemblage points to the need for supporting youth's literacy practices and the creation of alternative media in today's participatory cultures. First, a look at the "translocal" from an interdisciplinary perspective is key.

Translocal Assemblage

To understand translocal assemblage, I return to the notion of remix within DIY and DIT production discussed in chapters 1 and 2. The term remix, as borrowed from Lessig (2008), means to appropriate, borrow, and blend cultural texts to create new (or newer) texts and make them relevant again. At the heart of remix is the use of one or more modalities (oral or written language, images, symbols, sounds, gestures, artifacts, etc.) in specific semiotic domains that communicate distinctive types of meaning. Remix is not simply about a change in content (a derivative) but also a change in context (a different meaning). For example, young people draw on their knowledge of popular cultural texts to make meaning of other texts through processes of recontextualization. In other words, there is a process of differentiation, appropriation, translation, and the reframing of cultural material across symbolic forms and social practices (Dyson 2003). The reframing, which in itself is a remix, produces a different meaning. This line of thinking is certainly not new. Remix has been a term used in music to refer to a rewriting of sound, a kind of sampling with found objects where "the constraints get thin (and) the mix breaks free of the old associations" (Miller 2004, 25).

Remix as a form of layering echoes the translocal process of creation, particularly in extending activism and cultural politics among the hiphop generation (Chang 2005; Kitwana 2002; Rose 1994). For some educators, the translocal in remixing sound, image, and knowledge has been central to invigorating teaching and learning through culturally responsive pedagogy (Akom 2009; Dimitriadis 2001; Emdin 2010; Hill 2009; Love 2012; Morrell and Duncan-Andrade 2002; Richardson 2006; Stovall 2006b; Tinson and McBride 2013). More to the point, what is new in remix is the idea that young people in contemporary times are blurring genres of alternative media by building on each other's work and using technologies as dialogical tools of power to combat racial injustice, surveillance, and police brutality, among other things. The forging of cultural texts as found in multimedia poems and other genres of alternative media has implications for pedagogical innovations in education.

Adding to these perspectives on remix, the term *translocal* within literacy studies has been theorized in various ways. Scholars have pointed to the limits of the local and asserted the material consequences associated with literacy at a more global level (Brandt and Clinton 2002). Others have viewed artifacts as central to literacy research and have suggested the importance of attending to the material consequences that artifacts bear in the social world. For example, Braynham and Prinsloo (2009) trace the objects that circulate within and between sites of social human interaction as "things" that are seen as necessary components of social networks and practices (also see Latour 2005). This is similar to what Lam (2009) and Medina (2010) discuss as translocal literacy practices among youth in a digitally mediated world and the cultural flows that happen through migration and media exchange. Examples such as instant messaging and reading literature in transnational contexts are not only artifactual but also build on cultural imaginaries toward learning and literacy development (see also Medina and Wohlwend 2014). It has also been argued that, in grassroots literacies, texts produced in local economies become translocal documents with different possible uptakes (Blommaert 2008).

More specific to remix in youth cultural production and participatory politics, translocal assemblage (McFarlane 2009) offers an analytic frame for place-based social movements with the following:

1. An exchange of ideas, knowledge, practices, materials, and resources across sites;
2. An extension of connections between other groups or places in the movement beyond a node or point in history;
3. A building of relations between and within sites that signify a doing or performance but at the same time are open to collapse or to reassembling in other forms.

In other words, translocal assemblage provides a way to understand the production and dissemination of youth media work toward the exchange of ideas and knowledge, connections, and performance as action. As noted in the examples below, remix as an appropriation of existing texts to create new ones or the rewriting of the familiar is central to the process. The multimedia poems featured here display layers of intertextuality that signal a kind of assembling or (re)assembling of cultural material across space and time, an artifactual process of recontextualization in engaging cultural imaginaries. Theoretically, the intertextual or modally braided nature of media production opens up doors for exchange with similar yet different possible uptakes. Pedagogically, by building on existing media products, it renders the convergence of cultural material as part of translocal assemblage. For me, the college classroom provided a context for an instantiation of translocal assemblage in furthering the discourse on racial justice and related issues. The multimedia poems became integral in the discussion and production of alternative media.

Translocal Experiences of a Teacher-Learner

To understand the translocal is to be transparent about the pedagogical process. As the instructor of the new media literacies course described in chapter 4, I was a part of shaping the classroom context and the exchange of ideas on which the social action projects produced at the end of the semester were based. With my research and teaching interests in literacy and digital media technology, I received (and still do) lots of information about trending youth media via my social networks. In the fall of 2013, a multimedia poem called "Black Bruins" went viral on YouTube and landed on my Facebook page and Twitter feed. I was in southern California at the time, as mentioned in the opening scene of this chapter. I watched the video multiple times and was able to follow its trend over the next two months. I was intrigued by the use of spoken word poetry and the braiding of written, oral, and visual dimensions of production in the multimedia poem (Hull and Nelson 2005). Drawing on classroom inquiry and action research (Cochran-Smith and Lytle 1993), I utilized web sphere search and analysis to study web objects and their mediated patterns (Schneider and Foot 2005). This methodological approach allowed me to monitor the multimedia poem's trending effects on Facebook and Twitter, news media, and ensuing related media coverage.

Upon my return to class a few days after discovering the multimedia poem, I introduced it to students and, not to my surprise, several of my students had already seen it and passed it along to others in their social media networks. This goes to show the speed and degree of dispersion toward visibility at which the multimedia poem traveled (boyd 2014). With web sphere search and my continuous monitoring of "Black Bruins," I eventually came across another multimedia poem called "Black Beavers" and noticed right away the similarities across the productions. Material and cultural resources I gathered for class included links to both videos, the written text provided on each YouTube page, published articles or blogs, and other news media coverage. I proceeded to perform a content multimodal analysis of the videos in order to examine the idiosyncratic uptakes in both multimedia poems. The analysis included genre, actors/participants, content, context/locale, and stylistic choices of the producer (see Appendix A).

In the semester that followed, I proceeded to build on my initial analysis with a different cohort of students. It was not the first time I had utilized youth-produced works to facilitate thinking in my classroom. It was, however, my first time explicitly documenting and analyzing the translocal process of creation and production of alternative media alongside students. The fluid boundaries between teacher and learner shaped our interactions as members of the class. Methodologically, the dynamic teacher/student relationship enabled me as teacher to take the position of learner, and vice versa, and to further inform the translocal assemblage unfolding before us. I was learning alongside students as they shared interpretations of the multimedia poems and related examples we viewed together in class while I documented the pedagogical process. It did not take long to realize that our exchange of ideas and capacity building was shaping a kind of translocal assemblage in our classroom.

Both multimedia poems ("Black Bruins" and "Black Beavers") served as catalysts for in-class discussions and subsequently as models for students' digital storytelling and social action projects. For me, it was a deliberate attempt to draw on alternative media produced and distributed by university students themselves that focused on intersectionalities based on markers of difference such as race, gender, and institutional affiliations so that my own students would be able to see the potential impact of their own work. As noted previously, the pedagogical design necessitated careful attention to cohort and context (Luke, Woods, and Weir 2013). This meant selecting material relevant to students and engaging in activities that not only invigorated the curriculum about new media literacies but also promoted a kind of critical education that was mindful of our own positionings at the university in relation to the broader community.

In this classroom context, I was privileged as a teacher-learner to direct the co-construction of knowledge and curriculum-making for a particular purpose. My students went to work and considered the exemplary videos in their process. The multimedia poems ("Black Bruins" and "Black Beavers") led to brainstorming ideas and eventually the formation of small groups to address a particular educational or social issue toward the final social action project. The latter was enabled by conversations about race, gender, class, educational equity, and social inequities that affect young people or communities within the local context (Jocson, 2015a; also see discussion in chapter 4). Such construction of knowledge and curriculum-making in the classroom, I argue, are key to translocal assemblage.

Multimedia Poems on Race, Gender, and Representation

The objective of the social action project in the New Media Literacies class was to raise awareness on an educational or a social issue through the creation of short video documentaries. In class, we viewed and discussed two multimedia poems. One was UCLA student Sy Stokes's "Black Bruins," released in early November 2013, that triggered renewed conversations about the underrepresentation of African American students at major American universities, college admissions, and affirmative action. The multimedia poem sparked attention from news media (including local and national newspapers, television, and blogs); it also pushed university administrators at UCLA to address issues of racial climate on campus through organized panels and town hall meetings. Stokes appeared on several news media outlets expounding on the topic of underrepresentation and invisibility of Black students at the university.

In addition to such news coverage, the multimedia poem also shaped discourses nationwide. A similar multimedia poem, "Black Beavers," by Oregon State University's Anderson DuBoise III was released in early December 2013. The latter, in my view and as part of my argument here, is a form of remix. Subsequently, several other productions (video documentaries and the like) addressing the underrepresentation and experiences of racialized minority students at the university have added to an increasingly growing conversation (see "33" video and "I, Too, Am Harvard" campaign). Together, these productions point to understanding, on the one hand, youth's participation in the new media landscape and, on the other hand, the ways in which translocal practices of writing/performing and producing text—a "thing" reified through practice—travel from local to distant contexts (Brandt and Clinton 2002), only to be assembled or reassembled for new or similar purposes. Intertextuality is present in each of the multimedia poems. The use of statistical data and historical narratives drawn from various sources are also evident to localize issues and promote a message of racial justice. Each multimedia poem with its respective YouTube page is described below.

"Black Bruins"

On the "Black Bruins" YouTube page, the introductory text followed by production credits and lyrics provides a sense of the collaborative and intertextual nature of the production. The "Black Bruins" video has a total running time of 5:12. The point of view of the video centers on Sy Stokes with eleven other African American male students who stand staggered on steps in the background. All are wearing sweatshirts with a university logo; some are hooded and some are crew neck in style. Sy Stokes begins with the following:

> In fall 2012, the total enrollment, graduate and undergraduate, for African American males at UCLA was 660 students. That's 3.3% of the 19,838 other males enrolled here. Out of that 660 African American male students, 65% are undergraduate athletes. The number of entering male freshman students was 2,418; only 48 of them are African American. The graduation rates for African American males at UCLA is 74% . . . which means out of that 48 freshmen last year . . . only 35 are predicted to graduate.

Statistical data frames the issue of underrepresentation of African American students and their experiences on the university campus. The video goes on to elaborate the data in relation to past and contemporary history. The video begins with white text on black screen, noting the assassination of UCLA students and members of the Black Panther Party on campus in 1969. It ends with Sy Stokes saying, "So with all of my brothers' hopes and dreams that this university has tried to ruin/ How the hell am I supposed to be proud . . . to call myself. . . a Bruin." At this end point, all participants take off their sweatshirts and the video fades to black.

Apart from the video, the Comments section on the YouTube page published on November 4, 2013, included notes from Sy about a misspelled word, being related to Arthur Ashe, and the impetus for the production:

> Yes, I am aware that palettes is spelled wrong. I already uploaded the video when I saw the typo lol thx for paying so much attention!
> Being the cousin of Arthur Ashe, I feel as though it is my responsibility to uphold the strong voices of the Black Bruin community. This school has experienced unacceptable instances of injustice recently, and many people are not aware of what is happening at this university. I am a proud Black, Cherokee, and Chinese student at UCLA. Thank you for watching.

At the time of this writing, the video had been viewed over 2 million times.

"Black Beavers"

On the "Black Beavers" YouTube page, the layout and text structure are identical to "Black Bruins." The introductory text followed by production credits and lyrics provide a sense of the collaborative and intertextual nature of the production. Anderson DuBoise III is featured along with four other African American male students who also stand staggered on steps. All four are wearing hooded sweatshirts with a university logo. The "Black Beavers" video, published on December 11, 2013, has a total running time of 4:18. At the time of this writing, the video had been viewed over 13,000 times. Anderson DuBoise III begins with the following:

> At Oregon State University there is a total of 27,925 students, of that number there are only 366 black students which makes us 1.3% of the OSU population. There are 14,897 male identified students. Of those 14,897 there are only 201 African American men on this campus which makes up .7% of the population.

It becomes apparent quickly that "Black Beavers" is a response to and a remix of "Black Bruins." The text atop the YouTube page explicitly names "Black Bruins" and makes a reference to IGNITE (an acronym mentioned in the "Black Bruins" video that stands for Increasing Graduations, Not Incarcerations, Transforming Education). The direct acknowledgment of the issues raised in "Black Bruins" not only demonstrates translocal allegiance but also clear-cut writing of the politicized/ing (collective) self in the new media landscape. This point is evident in the following text:

> This is a response video to the UCLA Black Bruins letting them know we feel where they are coming from. Here at Oregon State University, the total Black student population makes up only 1.3% of the total student body. Nationally, the graduation rate for Black males is 33%. Recent research shows that there are more Black men going to college than prisons. However, we need to graduate. So let's IGNITE! Shout out to Sy Stokes for taking the lead! We have your back!

Analyzing the Multimedia Poems

Issues of underrepresentation and invisibility at one particular university (UCLA) transcend the local context and are recontextualized in another (Oregon State University). A new text was created as a derivative with a different meaning. Analysis of both multimedia poems suggests idiosyncratic uptakes that represent the local, yet the cultural imaginaries (or the collective vision of idealized communities) render the translocal. The similarities in the two multimedia poems include:

- the use of spoken word poetry and video (genre);
- the presence of Black male students (participants);
- the discourse about race in admissions, recruitment, and retention (content);
- the university setting and shot location (context or locale);
- the aesthetic and technical aspects of filmmaking, including cinematic and sound effects (stylistic choices).

As a response to the video "Black Bruins," "Black Beavers" is an appropriation of an already existing text (re)assembled in a new context. It represents a kind of remix across genre, participants, content, locale, and stylistic choices that together emerge as a translocal assemblage.

In other words, "Black Beavers" becomes a place-based social movement that draws on (1) an exchange of ideas, knowledge, practices, and resources across sites, (2) the capacity to extend and exceed connections between groups or places, and (3) shifting relations within and between the sites that signify a doing for future reassembling (McFarlane 2009). A reference at the end of the lyrics section on the YouTube page says, "So to the Black Bruins of UCLA, we feel you, and to the dark voices yet unspoken around the nation, we hear you." Apparent in this last line of the poem is a firm recognition of critical solidarity (or a social commitment to alliance) to make a larger statement about race in admissions and the underrepresentation of Black students at two major universities. It marks cultural imaginaries taking shape across contexts.

Putting It All Together in the Classroom

In August of 2014, Ferguson, Missouri, was front and center in news outlets and social media. Michael Brown, an unarmed Black eighteen year old, was killed by White police officer Darren Wilson. Brown was shot at least seven times and his body was left in the street for four hours before it was removed. The events in Ferguson over time shaped national and global protests against police brutality and racial violence against Black and Brown youth. Many of the protests were organized and led by youth themselves using #Ferguson (Bonilla and Rosa 2015). Examples of participatory politics included the use of Facebook, Twitter, and Instagram with hashtags, photographs, and video footage to accompany messages of justice, solidarity, and social action. While it is difficult to predict trends in social media, events that occurred prior to Michael Brown's killing in Ferguson provided some sense of what had been brewing nationally and globally through participatory politics (including the election of President Obama, Arab Spring, the Occupy Movement, and Kony 2012).

My students and I were aware of recent events specific to racial justice that dominated social media, such as the killing of Trayvon Martin and the case of George Zimmerman. In the spring of 2014, I along with students explored contemporary perspectives on new media and culture while pushing ourselves to put to work new media literacies. The majority of the students ranged from ages 19 to 22. As part of the course, we read and discussed scholarship on theories and practices of new media literacies (see Kellner and Share 2007; Lankshear and Knobel 2006; Lister et al. 2009). We also explored alternative and activist new media to advance our thinking on the transformative potential of new media literacies. For example, it is argued that alternative and activist new media "employ or modify the communication artifacts, practices, and social arrangements of new and information and communication technologies to challenge or alter dominant, expected, or accepted ways of doing society, culture, and politics" (Lievrouw 2011, 19).

Genres of alternative and activist new media include culture jamming, participatory journalism, alternative computing, mediated mobilization, and commons knowledge. As discussed in chapter 4 and important to reiterate here, we saw our engagement with DIY and DIT production as falling under the categories of culture jamming, participatory journalism, and commons knowledge. Students blogged and shared related work viewable online by the public. Central to Lievrouw's argument is mediation, or the continuous and mutual reshaping of "the relationship between people's uses of technology and their communicative action that produces social and technological change" (231). This point in our thinking was important to further our analysis of the multimedia poems we had viewed, the production of digital storytelling and social action projects, and translocal assemblage.

Over time, we engaged readings on critical media pedagogy (Morrell et al. 2013), popular culture and teaching in urban schools (Mahiri 2006; Philip and Garcia 2013), youth media (Jocson, 2013a; Soep 2011; Vasudevan 2010), and copyright and fair use in education (Hobbs and Donnelly 2011). Evident in the teaching and learning process was the assembling or reassembling of ideas that enabled connections beyond one node in history. Translocal assemblage was embedded in the pedagogy as much as it was in the media production that followed. While it was a privilege to be a part of that classroom, it was also affirming to notice that some aspects of youth media as assemblage (remix), as critical solidarity (alliance), as place-making (situatedness), and as pedagogy (teaching and learning) came together to mark a space of possibility.

I believe the approach to studying and applying new media literacies in our work enabled certain ways of thinking and doing. However, what it enabled is not unique to us. I argue that youth media further conceptualized as assemblage, critical solidarity, place-making, and pedagogy can be meaningfully repurposed in a wide variety of educational settings. I also argue that when teaching and learning processes are viewed as dynamic (not as static or technical) the potential for transformative DIY and DIT production is likely and can be guided by those involved, inclusive of youth and adult participants. This is important as we forge ahead, make pedagogic moves in the classroom, and look to youth media for examples within participatory cultures. Whether in school or beyond, youth media offers a way of understanding media production and distribution as a particular form of youth resistance and an age-old practice of storytelling renewed into a theory of change (Tuck and Yang 2014).

Assemblage, Critical Solidarity, Place-Making, and Pedagogy

Youth are taking up issues and lifting up voices of dissent in the fast changing new media landscape. Now more than ever, it is important to pay attention to the link between youth cultural production, translocal assemblage, and critical solidarity as youth position themselves at the center of dialogue. Youth bring to bear their social worlds as a form of place-making, and we ought to listen, watch, and learn. As critical educators interested in innovating curriculum and pedagogy, it is imperative to open up learning opportunities in the classroom and to make connections for more meaningful learning experiences. We must consider what it would mean to build on youth cultural production and the plurality of voices to set off new ideas, as young people continue to share knowledge across space, time, and matter. We must also consider how young people connect to build on each other's works, blur different genres of alternative media, and speak back to power in shaping discourses about race, racism, race relations, and racial justice. This view asserts that digital media technology platforms such as YouTube extend dialogic tools of power in and out of the classroom.

Many examples on social media build on translocal assemblage practices. In 2014, experimental videos, short documentaries, and other genres were produced and disseminated that, as argued here, took shape in part because of what "Black Bruins" incited and what ensued with the production of "Black Beavers." Some examples include "33," a video produced by Black students at UCLA School of Law, this time focused on the racialized experiences of graduate students.[2] "I, Too, Am Harvard," a photo campaign by Black students at Harvard College, demonstrates a way of speaking back to whiteness and the persistence of White supremacy in society to highlight students' voices about racialized experiences across geographic lines.[3] These works reflect cultural flows as fluid and dynamic. Materially and discursively, these works are indicative of translocal assemblage that points to the exchange of ideas, knowledge, practices, materials, and resources across sites (McFarlane 2009; 2012), and the ways in which the connections between them and the potential for reassembling cultural material into different forms of alternative media can be relevant to teaching, learning, and critical education (Cohen et al. 2012; Soep 2014). Young people are finding civic resources and telling stories about their political becoming. That requires designing learning environments that support the envisioning of cultural imaginaries and the making of public spheres.

The examples described throughout this book continue to push our thinking about how youth are coming together in local–distant contexts, participating in the new media landscape, and inserting themselves more actively online and offline to raise awareness about issues that are relevant in their lives. Some become more visible than others, which may pave the way more quickly for other forms of remix and cultural flows. This is not to say that all youth engage (or will engage) in media production or have exchanges about cultural material to promote social awareness, however fleeting those exchanges may be. The point is that cultural material is produced (often in a thoughtful manner) and made available for a wide audience to access. Some youth interested in particular issues or topics of the day will take up that cultural material to be (re)assembled in new ways. It has been reported that the majority of youth are not engaged in participatory politics (Cohen et al. 2012). Many do not automatically conceive of creating something for the public good, yet, as I have argued here, can be prompted to do so with the support of peers and adults in their lives. This is why youth media as assemblage, as critical solidarity, as place-making, and as pedagogy are all the more important. Indeed, youth are using digital media technology with different tools for different purposes across educational settings.

With an understanding of the relational impact of new technologies on teaching and learning, it is imperative to see youth media's potential to move us toward transformative education. *How can we as educators and youth advocates create the kinds of spaces, practices, and conditions toward educative possibilities that can have real and tangible social impact?* In thinking about possible answers to this question, educators and youth advocates must also participate in the making and remaking of cultural imaginaries, a kind of public pedagogy (Giroux 2004) that extends *the who* and *the how* of pedagogy to the ways in which the cultural-political (Youdell 2011) can be intertwined in the daily life of school and other educational contexts. This is more crucial than ever as we see increasing levels of participatory politics among youth. The translocal links different forms of struggle and politics of difference in cultural and social movements, where the translocal becomes part of transnational discourses, and vice versa.

Multimedia poems and other forms of media production offer young people ways of writing the politicized/ing (collective) self. As we have witnessed, many youths are drawing on their voices and talents to challenge normalized discourses, disrupt dominant narratives and power structures, and act as concerned members of society. Specifically, they are performing identities, allegiances, and oppositions that reach wide audiences. Since the writing of this book, many more examples of alternative media have emerged that engage in communicative action and mobilize the public concerning race relations, racism, and racial justice. Mass protests in the Black Lives Matter movement, for example, have awakened a new generation of activists (Taylor 2016). The movement is alive and online. At the forefront are collectives such as the Black Youth

Project (BYP 100) that aim to use direct action organizing and education in conjunction with #blacklivesmatter.[4]

It is no accident that varied groups across locales have come together as part of a historical continuum to remix cultural material with a commitment to social alliance and social action. Alternative media does not just surface because more and more young people are engaging in participatory politics. Tactics of participatory politics such as creating and circulating information via social media platforms often require a continuous process of mediation between people's uses of technology and communicative action that can push social and cultural change in certain directions (Lievrouw 2011; Soep 2014). Critical arts and media-based literacy pedagogies play an integral part in youth's civic engagement (Rogers et al. 2015). As I have illustrated in this chapter and in earlier examples, alternative media in the form of multimedia poems incited the exchange of ideas and capacity building to (re)assemble cultural material into different genres of participatory politics. The translocal practice of young people building on each other's work was mediated by the need to respond to locally unjust social arrangements and the need to come together discursively as a form of social alliance. There are many other educative moments and spaces of possibility that can enable a kind of connected learning focused on equity and justice-oriented approaches in and beyond the classroom.

Directions for Research and Practice

Researching youth media is no different from any critical inquiry that seeks to use research to combat forms of inequity. The inquiry entails a process of humanization that is mutually constitutive for participants and researchers. More important, the inquiry yields altered views of youth as knowledge producers and as active members of society in an increasingly participatory culture. As Paris and Winn (2014) point out, the research act becomes humanizing as youth provide researchers access to understanding their world. The research act involves building relationships and creating terrains of exchange to confront multiple borders of difference. That is, interactions between youth participants and researchers are shaped by their willingness to share life experiences uncommon in traditional research. In my own work, these interactions have gifted me with a more informed lens to understand youth media across educational settings. Youth media is a cultural and educational movement; studying what young people create and share as linked to their everyday experience has implications for research and practice.

Toward Critical Media Ethnography

In the past decades, critical ethnography has influenced the way educational researchers and other social scientists conduct studies with and for communities. The shift toward new historical movements in qualitative research has expanded existing approaches. This section builds upon what critical ethnographers have put forth as doing research that seeks to better the social conditions of participants in particular settings. Critical ethnography frames the approach, while youth media offers an area of inquiry through which to examine young people's consumption, production, and distribution of cultural material. Along with my role as teacher-researcher-collaborator, what I point out are uses of digital media that attend to and challenge cultural representations of youth in new media times. I note the importance of visuality in video production and multimedia composition. On one hand, the visual affords layered meanings in representation and allows creators to lace image with sound and printed text through the use of digital technologies. On the other, the visual implies transparency and identification that may reinforce the dominant gaze on racialized and minoritized groups—in this case, youth of color and youth from low-income backgrounds. The implications of digitality and visuality are significant to researching youth media.

Throughout my work in literacy and urban education, I have espoused a critical ethnographic approach. Critical ethnography is no different from conventional ethnography in that it relies on qualitative methods and interpretation of data. It is inductive in nature and often leads to the development of grounded theory (Glaser and Strauss, 1967). Critical ethnography, however, draws on critical methodology that resists the domestication of truth; it is based on critical epistemology, not on value orientation (Carspecken, 1996). It moves away from "what is" to "what could be" in the commitment to address processes of injustice within particular lived domains and toward human freedom. The art of fieldwork and the recognition of subjective human experience along with local knowledge and vernacular expressions adhere to the postmodern turn or new movements in qualitative research (Denzin, 2001, 2003; Noblit, Flores, and Murrillo, 2004). For critical ethnographers, it is important to attend to one's positionality and dialogue with the Other (Fine 1994; Madison 2005). Critical ethnography is also about conducting rigorous research to invoke a call to action and to use knowledge for social change (Thomas, 1993).

As my interest in youth media grew, so did my approach to research. The demands of qualitative research made explicit my subjective role as teacher-researcher and often as a participant-collaborator doing critical ethnography. It was important to be attentive to my own positionalities and subjectivities. Equally important was considering how processes of media production construct as well as communicate particular narratives, which may or may not be deserved by the subject institutions like schools and universities. The colonial project of formal schooling has been historically damaging to racialized and minoritized groups, and it is a project that remains intact (perhaps doubly damaging in today's digital age if not questioned or challenged). Indigenous scholars note this colonial project as akin to research being dirty and operating within a flawed theory of change (Smith 1999; Tuck 2009). Apart from the rigidity of schooling and related social structures, a kind of undoing or pausing to rethink the colonial genealogies of research is necessary to interrupt what has been and see what *can* be in the future. The latter demands a practice of answerability (Patel 2016). My pausing is as much about learning, unlearning, and relearning, to be answerable to the young people with whom I have worked, the communities in which they are situated, and the media they have produced time and time again. I have begun to call this aspect of my work critical media ethnography.

Digitality and Visuality

The examples in this book illustrate opportunities for constructing narratives mediated by youth's experiences. However, the nature of some of the videos identified and documented intimate aspects of youths' lives. It is possible that their likenesses, reified through photographs, video sequences, and texts branded with real names, may yield some unintended effects. This was particularly significant in chapter 1, where concerns about digitality and visuality surfaced. In historically marginalized communities, the penetration into the private lives of students and their families as a potential outcome of research must be taken with serious consideration.

In my view as a critical media ethnographer, revealing research participants' likenesses without consideration of potential risks would be irresponsible and unethical. In other words, it is essential to take into account identification (of names and locations), documentation (of faces and bodies), and representation (of individuals and groups) in multimedia projects. In writing up research and (re)constructing narratives, I make a conscious choice to disseminate information with an unknown audience in a much more careful manner. In the case of delicate subject matter, it is necessary to be cognizant of real names appearing in beginning and ending credits, as well as photographs of home addresses, neighborhoods, landmarks, and street names. Is this concern for identification, documentation, and representation a new phenomenon in qualitative research? Or is it similar to what appeared in visual anthropology, only now with the use of more advanced technological tools? And what are the implications for educational research? More to the point, what are the implications for literacy education and literacy research, specifically for emerging studies in new media literacies and participatory cultures?

The issue is neither to note the changing nature of media technologies nor to disregard what technological tools have to offer research. Researchers have anticipated these changes and now know some baseline trends in literacy and digital media technology. New forms of literacy research employing qualitative methods open up spaces, discourses, and lines of inquiry, including arts-based, digital, and geographical analyses (Albers, Holbrook, and Flint 2014). Instead, the issue is about ethics and sensibilities in doing research, a kind of answerability to the research participants with whom the researcher is inextricably linked. The nature of digitality and visuality in youth media production is such that it often reveals the likeness of those involved. It is the responsibility of the researcher to conceal as much as possible the identities and affiliations of participants if the media product may pose possible risks to their academic (school), career (work), and social (family and peer network) life trajectories. This holds true for young people as well who publish revealing content about themselves and sometimes their politics, and later discover the need to employ tactics of participatory politics to protect their public and private lives (Soep 2014). The researcher in these shifting times of digital media must contend with different possibilities, good or bad. It is difficult to foresee potential risks, yet the responsibility still falls in the researcher's hands.

More and more educators are embracing the use of video and other types of media production in their classrooms. The practice demands researchers (including teacher-collaborators) to consider the implications of representing student products depicting personal material as well as their likenesses on the page and on the screen. What potential harm does public dissemination of youth-produced media and other cultural material render? What is the purpose and who is the intended audience? Depending on the nature of the video composition, the representation of certain segments and sequences may be limited, for example, to purposeful abstractions through the blurring of faces or removal of names. In treating entire videos with care, it may be necessary to include representations in the analysis but exclude them in the visual reporting. Perhaps research studies that examine similar phenomena in youth media and cultural production may seek other types of analysis or ways of reporting. Perhaps they may not require the level of attention and care I am noting. Perhaps the idea of refusing research (Simpson 2007; Tuck and Yang, 2014) or withdrawing from sharing information altogether may just be the best option.

As research in youth media in participatory cultures expands, so will our approaches, methods, and analyses. These might include design-based and ecological approaches, as we have seen in previous chapters. Such approaches do not preclude practitioners from also engaging in teacher inquiry or action research to examine their own classrooms in shaping possible learning environments. Some consideration of who is served and for what purposes is central to expanding possibilities, particularly in today's growing maker movement (Vossoughi, Hooper, and Escudé, 2016). Using a cultural lens and addressing the sociopolitical contexts of our classrooms and other educative sites becomes all the more important. That said, I am reminded of the affordances of new media, the theorizing of new literacies, and the application of new media literacies that enable researchers to be more thoughtful about conducting studies with and for various communities (Morrell et al. 2013; Sanford, Rogers, and Kendrick 2014; Williams and Zenger 2012).

Critical media ethnography with its emphasis on digitality and visuality are shaping new questions. For example, in what ways is critical media ethnography similar to or different from other methodological approaches? In what ways do value orientations play a part in the research process? What are the epistemological issues that must be considered? If full reporting cannot be achieved, then what can researchers offer the research community in terms of validity and transparency? In what ways can the objects of study involving multiple modes be known and inscribed? Should they be? How does ideology influence the apprehension of meaning? Is the latter even possible?

In pausing, I am struck by the entangled complexities and contingencies in meaning-making that sometimes result in simplified explanations (Patel 2016). The simultaneous making, unmaking, and remaking of meaning is layered with textures from multiple angles. As Leonardo and Allen (2008) point out, representations in qualitative research are partial, and ideological differences between researchers and participants may guide what is constructed and translated from empirical sources. Thinking with theory may offer ways of hearing participants' voices not simply as they are but as contingent upon various material and discursive factors (Jackson and Mazzei 2012). This is a consideration as well for what participants produce and what is uttered within their productions. Despite the many possibilities in youth media, I believe it is crucial to pause and rethink the implications for research. It is my hope that such ideas enable more robust conversations about the who, the why, and the how of critical inquiry. Embracing digitality and visuality will require a more sophisticated lens through which to understand the human experience and the multiplicities in cultural imaginaries.

Now What?

Youth media as assemblage, as critical solidarity, as place-making, and as pedagogy tells us a little something about what young people (and the adults working with them) are already doing with information and communication technologies. The stories threaded in media production, braided by multiple modes and steeped in everyday experiences, illuminate the very reasons youth media matters—and why youth media continues to matter in participatory cultures. The stories, of course, did not just come into being in isolation. The stories were a cultural, material, and human remix of sorts that brought together young people to break open genres of expression. The stories were real and situated in place.

The locality of uptakes provided a clear view of how stories were linked to power and the tactics employed in media production and distribution to disrupt power structures.

There is no one way of reading or interpreting the cultural material. The entangled layers of texture are many. We can, however, try to learn in the making, unmaking, and remaking of meaning with students inside our classrooms and through everyday conversations. That is part of the pedagogy. Young people are drawing on new media literacies to make statements about place and uneven relations of power as they understand the world around them. And we are a part of shaping that world, with the utmost responsibility for shaping it with them. Perhaps the media produced and shared in classrooms and schools, in film festivals, on social media, and in other youth-centered spaces will inspire and once again trigger new(er) ideas.

It has been a gift to be able to teach courses at the university and collaborate with teachers in high school classes where we attend to issues of equity and social justice in education. I have learned a ton and have shared those lessons in this book. The dynamics of learning are often shaped by the very people and cultural practices brought into the classrooms, and the social locations from where they come. Of late, my graduate students and I find pleasure in collectively contributing to the teaching and learning that happens. It is not uncommon to bring to each class multimedia examples, including songs, poems, videos, visual art, and websites relevant to our work. It is also not uncommon to produce content using digital media technology. I say this because media production within participatory cultures is not just for or with "youth" (high school and college students aged 15–24). For me, youth media is just as relevant to the molding of the next generation of educators and researchers interested in working with young people. It goes without saying that building rapport with young people is one thing; getting them to trust or believe in you is another. Examining youth media has been a way to understand the various spaces of possibility afforded by the exchange of ideas or inspired stories available online. Digital storytelling, PSAs, short videos, podcasts, and interactive websites are now common ingredients of my current teaching practice. I believe that these ingredients can be further modified and particularized for work with future students.

So far, I have shown youth media from multiple lenses and in a range of contexts. This book is an attempt to bridge different perspectives to help move the field of education forward. In short, there is no one way to engage in media production. Young people find ways on their own and with each other to cultivate their academic, creative, and social interests. Those interests can often lead to spaces of possibility. For educators, it is important to invigorate the curriculum in ways that further support spaces of possibility in and beyond classrooms. As illustrated by examples throughout this book, young people are building on their talents and experiences to craft stories that are relevant in their lives, their families, and their communities. We need to bolster our work in literacy education more broadly. Literacy happens not just in content area classrooms but across educational settings. Young people as savvy as some of them are with digital media technology still require mentorship and guidance from educators to support higher-order thinking, critical engagement, and opportunities for critical design literacy in content-world creation (Soep 2014; Watkins 2012).

Young people need opportunities to cultivate new media literacies, especially as they immerse themselves in sophisticated practices involving networked publics (boyd 2014). Media production is one means of merging repertoires of cultural practice with the core competencies of new media literacies. Media production enables youth to participate more fully in school and society, to be more visible in the new media landscape, and to construct versions of themselves in critical moments of becoming. We have to tune in. We can do more than give praise or celebrate. We can study and repurpose youth-produced media to help design courses. We can treat youth media as more than texts. We can embrace a pedagogy that takes seriously the very issues that matter in youth's lives to better the world we live in. We can follow, share, and retweet youth media work. We have so much to gain when we are willing to open ourselves by asking what *can* be toward transformative education.

Analyzing Media Texts

	TECHNICAL	CONCEPTUAL	AESTHETIC
Script	How long is the written text? What are the characteristics upon recording (e.g., tone, pitch, volume)? Is there copyright involved?	What is the logic of the text? Does it carry throughout? Is the purpose of the text clear? What message is being conveyed?	What are the stylistic choices in depicting the script/voice (e.g., tone, pitch, and volume)? What mood do these choices create aurally?
Image	What images are included? How many? From where are images retrieved or collected? Is there copyright involved?	Who/what is represented? Who/what is not? Why? What's the logic behind the sequencing? What is the purpose?	What are the stylistic choices in depicting the image(s)? What mood do these choices create visually?
Sound	What sound is included? How long is it? Does it need modification based on the length of the script? Is there copyright involved?	What types of sound, song, or beat accompany the voice-text? How does it relate to the purpose? Who/what does it represent?	What are the stylistic choices in depicting the sound(s)? What mood do these choices create aurally?

Gathering Empirical Material: Methods and Analysis

In the ethnographic study conducted at Randall High School, data were drawn from multiple sources: pre- and post-survey about media technology and mapping; semi-structured student and teacher interviews; field notes from participant observations (in class, at school, at community partner sites); videotaping of class episodes and related events; photographs of events and places when videotaping was impossible; student literacy artifacts (drafts and final versions, print and digital); students' report cards and attendance records; teacher curricular materials including syllabi and lesson plans; and school district and state-level data reports. The data corpus included 119 pages of interview transcriptions, 104 pages of transcribed class episodes or group sessions, 546 photographs, 115 pages of field notes, 5 scripts in final form (along with copies of multiple drafts), 5 op-ed videos including slideshows (plus multiple outtakes), and 1 QuickTime movie of the "Put Us on the Map" broadcast.

Content and visual analysis of various texts in the data yielded emerging patterns in the production process. For example, content analysis of interviews, field notes, and class episodes focused on *what participants said* in real time while visual analysis of photographs and videos focused on *what and how participants compositionally illustrated* their selected topics in representational mode (Rose 2007). Analysis began with open coding to establish categories of place as a source of learning and place as material. It was important to consider the learning ecology in segmenting the data (Strauss and Corbin 1998). The learning ecology consisting of various specific places (i.e., classroom and classroom television studio, school auditorium and athletic field, school district television station) emerged as an intersection (Massey 2005), an axis of "meeting places," where people negotiate ways of relating with each other, with the places themselves, and with the technological tools.

At the television station, for example, it became apparent how place was shaping students' participation and simultaneously how students' participation was shaping the place while making it their own. Such material and ontological dimensions of place signaled the importance of difference and social relations (Nespor 2008) with students' experiences in the production process as fundamental to place-making.

Student Information Sheet

STUDENT NAME*	MAJOR AREA OF STUDY	RACE/ETHNICITY (SELF-DESIGNATED)	GENDER	LEVEL OF MEDIA PRODUCTION EXPERIENCE
Alvin	English	White	M	Intermediate
Amber	International Business; Educational Studies	Caucasian	F	None
Amy	American Culture Studies (graduate)	African American	F	None
Anna	Urban Studies	African American	F	Beginner
Devon	Urban Studies	African American	F	None
Danny	Education (graduate)	Korean American	M	Beginner
Eddie	International Business	White	M	None
Heather	Business: Organizational Behavior; Educational Studies	White	F	None
Jim	Business: Organizational Behavior; Healthcare Management	Caucasian	M	None
Janet	English Literature	White	F	Beginner
Kelly	Communication Design	Caucasian	F	Intermediate
Samantha	Educational Studies; Psychology; Children's Studies	White	F	None
Val	English Literature; Cultural Studies (graduate)	Thai American / White	M	None

*All names are pseudonyms.

FIGURE 8. *Student information sheet from first day of class.*

STUDENT NAME	REASON(S) FOR TAKING THE COURSE —Information Sheet [1/22/14]—	TAKE-AWAYS —Check-Out [4/23/14]—
Alvin	Interested in education, scope and influence of media as a persuasive tool (good and bad); I've never taken anything like this before.	I realize how pervasive new media is and the way certain people are privileged with different kinds of literacy. My role is worthy consumer but I hope to produce more.
Amber	I'm minoring in educational studies and this class seemed like something different and interesting. I expect to learn things that I have not been exposed to in other classes.	New media literacy shapes my views on culture, technology, and society. This class posed interesting questions that make me rethink my views.
Amy	I really am unfamiliar with the topic so I would love to learn more information. It seems like it could be really applicable to my career.	New media literacy is the way we view the world as digital beings at the intersection of the way we use technology. I love the open nature of the class. It provided a more inclusive dialogue.
Anna	Heard about the class and it sounds interesting and relevant to my major.	All of it makes me realize that our culture is dramatically shifting and how we need to change old ways of thinking.
Devon	I expect to learn how media can be used in the classroom to promote learning. I want to go into nonprofit management specifically dealing with education and learning effective and novel ways to teach students would probably help me later in my journey.	New media literacy has pushed me to see how I interact with new media as well as how it shapes what I see. It has shown that we are constantly expanding upon new media literacies and the interactions we have with them. The course was very interesting and a refreshing break from my usual school interactions. It allowed me to understand learning in a new way. The most interesting aspect was creating the social action video because it allowed me to apply new media literacies to something I am passionate about.

FIGURE 9. *Student responses on information sheet and check-out.*

STUDENT NAME	REASON(S) FOR TAKING THE COURSE — Information Sheet [1/22/14]—	TAKE-AWAYS —Check-Out [4/23/14]—
Danny	I am hoping that I will be able to use some of the materials and things from this class to help better my instruction and use of technology.	I learned that new media literacy is a living entity. It is constantly growing and changing as we evolve as a people. Utilizing these tools will always be a constant battle in my classroom to push my students to their full potential.
Eddie	This class is very different from my major, so I'm mostly just trying to learn some new information about a different study.	New media literacy makes me consider the footprint that everything I do leaves as well as the impact that media have on the world and what impacted them.
Heather	As an educational studies minor, I am really looking forward to learning about education in a new, more modern age. I think it will complement my other classes and help me learn more about the current methods.	New media literacy pushes me to constantly be thinking about how I can learn new things and be an active participant in this new, exciting age. I am looking forward to all the developments in the years to come.
Jim	Enjoyed the last class and needed more [upper] level course elective. Expect the class to be fun and interesting. Hope the workload is second semester senior appropriate (though that doesn't mean I'm going to do a second-semester senior–level job on the work).	The class really taught me that I can never stop learning. The world is constantly changing.
Janet	My high school has recently given every student an iPad. This has caused me to have several discussions with friends on this topic and has developed my interest in this subject.	New media literacy shapes my view of the world. How and where I obtain information daily shapes which way the info is presented to me.
Kelly	I'm really interested in education and the education system we have in the U.S. I'm also interested in how technology may be positively and negatively impacting our future (and current) generations. I hope to gain more insight into these topics. My dad works at an online education company— combining the two has piqued my interest.	New media literacy made me consider how I fit in amongst our generation and the upcoming generations. I think this class made me more aware of different sides of NML which have been helpful in forming a more rounded opinion. I loved the incorporation of the [larger] community, something so important yet not focused on here at [the university] enough.

STUDENT NAME	REASON(S) FOR TAKING THE COURSE — Information Sheet [1/22/14]—	TAKE-AWAYS —Check-Out [4/23/14]—
Samantha	I'm really interested in the way education is changing as technology rapidly advances. I think it seriously impacts the student experience, starting in preschool. I hope to learn more about that!	New media literacy is so relevant to much of how I think about culture and education. Understanding the concept of NML is integral to comprehending the way society functions and how we can contribute to it. I learned so much from each project. I genuinely enjoyed completing the assignments because they've challenged me to try new things and develop new skills and engage with new and different kinds of people.
Val	I'm interested in the complexity of the term "literacy." In a previous course on testing, politics, and science we discussed issues of accessibility, and how to accommodate testers with disabilities or for whom English isn't their primary language (and if the tests were administered in English). I have an interest in education and am considering putting together a program of study. I hope to learn how literacy and new media figure into today's classroom.	I now understand more concretely the importance of new media literacy, and the ubiquity of new media in everyday life. I appreciate the theoretical frameworks with which we explored the subject, and can identify more examples of new media literacy. Finally, I enjoyed the direction the course took with focusing on alternative and activist new media as a way of giving and/or finding voice. As we continue to strive to make education a means of improving the world around us, it is important to have perspectives that may sometimes be relegated to the margins incorporated in the conversation, and new media allows that.

Notes

1. Assemblage in Content Area Classrooms

1. See KQED Education at https://ww2.kqed.org/education. The site offers ideas and examples of multimedia content, student activities, and professional development tools for classroom use. Content areas include news and civics, arts, science, and language.

2. All interviews with teachers and students were conducted by me at Glen High School.

3. The idea of narrative assemblage resonates in many of today's classrooms. I begin chapter 1 with earlier work to demonstrate trajectories in my own research as well as the shifting times and technologies in line with classroom practice illustrated in later chapters.

2. Critical Solidarity in Literary and Media Arts

1. "Slip of the Tongue" is available at https://www.youtube.com/watch?v=z-yu-SZP7ew. "Barely Audible" is available at https://www.youtube.com/watch?v=UC-hQvBvAyY.

2. NAMAC became the Alliance in 2016. For more information on recent data and trends, see http://www.thealliance.media/resources/.

3. For a list of other programs, see Patricia Campbell-Kibler's "Sticking With My Dreams" at http://www.campbell-kibler.com/youth_media.pdf.

4. The use of the names as they appear in the credits of each video is deliberate. It recognizes the poet/writer and producer/filmmaker for their creative contributions. According to Soep and Chavez (2010), it is challenging enough for youth to fight for recognition in a high-powered field. The inclusion of real names is a careful but conscious move. Chapter 5 discusses some constraints that may arise from digitality and visuality in researching youth media.

5. All interviews with poets, artists, and producers were conducted by me.

6. See above link for "Slip of the Tongue." For Adriel's current works, visit http://drzzl.com/.

7. See above link for "Slip of the Tongue." For Karen's current works, visit http://www.womanlystateofmind.com/.

8. This segment was originally published as part of Jocson with Jacobs-Fantauzzi (2013),13–31.

9. See above link for "Barely Audible." For Chinaka's current works, visit http://chinakahodge.com/.

10. See above link for "Barely Audible." For Eli's current works, visit http://www.clenchedfistproductions.com/.

11. For example, Youth Voices is a social network started by a group of teachers from local sites of the National Writing Project (http://youthvoices.live). The website offers a way for teachers to share curriculum and ideas about digital literacies; it also encourages students to participate and publish their work.

3. Place-Making in Career and Technical Education

1. There are various studies featuring place-based approaches. It is not my intent here to distinguish pedagogical possibilities of place between local and global, formal and informal, or urban and rural settings; more important to this chapter are the affordances of place-based pedagogies to innovate curriculum that support underserved students from low socioeconomic and historically marginalized backgrounds.

2. According to Agnew (2011), place and space are fairly complex words that signal different understandings of "where" in relation to "when" and "how" something happens. It is outside the scope of this chapter to delineate the differences that reflect practices of philosophers, cartographers, and the sciences. Most important is place as a site in space that relates to other sites due to interaction, movement, and networks.

3. Such perspectives on place build on earlier works (see Massey 1984; 1994).

4. An extended treatment of place-based education is discussed in related works (Gruenewald 2003b, 2008; Smith and Gruenewald 2008; also see Bowers 2008; McInerney, Smyth, and Down 2011). Place-based perspectives in the arts and humanities also take up ecology in conjunction with pedagogy (see Ball and Lai 2006; Graham 2007).

5. All interviews with the teacher and participating students were conducted by me.

6. One of the topics (school closures) was explored later in the year. Due to a winning football season and playoff schedule, Lamar decided to join David in completing the segment on high school graduation rates.

7. This segment was originally published as part of Jocson 2015b.

4. Centrality of Pedagogy in the College Classroom

1. The university is a private research institution. Some students have referred to the university as a bubble that is removed from the larger community. Like many universities, however, there are opportunities for service learning and community engagement or other public service initiatives.

2. For more information, see www.newmedialiteracies.org .

3. For those interested in employing a similar approach, additional perspectives on digital storytelling and its various applications in youth-centered spaces include applied theater (Alrutz 2015), multilingual approaches (Anderson and Macleroy 2016), and pathways to learning and creativity (Ohler 2013). Other exam-

ples of multimodal and community-based inquiry projects might also be helpful (see Bruce, Bishop, and Budhathoki 2014; Vasudevan and DeJaynes 2013).

4. This segment was originally published as part of Jocson 2016b, 106–13.

5. All names are pseudonyms.

6. I informed students of my research interests in youth literacies and my ethical responsibilities as a qualitative researcher. A few weeks into the semester, permission was granted to me via written consent forms by a number of students whose digital stories were analyzed in more detail.

7. In order to accommodate project timelines, it became necessary to streamline assigned readings and modify the schedule of two group presentations. I felt compelled to have students spend more time with the inquiry given the short window toward the completion of the video documentaries and interactive websites.

8. The interactive websites had at least three tabs: the Homepage as a blog, an About page, and a Resources page. The Homepage contained the embedded video from YouTube. Visitors could post comments and access related information via links. WordPress, Tumblr, or Google Sites hosted the interactive websites.

5. Translocal Possibilities and the Politics of Media Making

1. "Black Bruins" is available at https://www.youtube.com/watch?v=BEO3 H5BOlFk. "Black Beavers" is available at https://www.youtube.com/watch?v =Nb6mXj9aenk.

2. "33" is available at https://www.youtube.com/watch?v=5y3C5KBcCPI.

3. "I, Too, Am Harvard" is available at http://itooamharvard.tumblr.com.

4. For more information, visit blackyouthproject.com and byp100.org.

Bibliography

Agnew, J. 2011. "Space and Place." In *Sage Handbook of Geographical Knowledge,* ed. J. Agnew and D. Livingstone. London: Sage.

Akom, A. A. 2009. "Critical Hip Hop Pedagogy as a Form of Liberatory Praxis." *Equity and Excellence in Education* 42, no. 1: 52–66.

Akom, A. A., J. Cammarota, and S. Ginwright. 2008. "Youthtopias: Towards a New Paradigm of Critical Youth Studies." *Youth Media Reporter* 2, no. 4: 1–30, http://www.youthmediareporter.org/2008/08/15/youthtopias-towards-a-new-paradigm-of-critical-youth-studies/.

Albers, P., T. Holbrook, and A. S. Flint, eds. 2014. *New Methods for Literacy Research.* New York: Routledge.

Alrutz, M. 2015. *Digital Storytelling, Applied Theatre, and Youth: Performing Possibility.* New York: Routledge.

Althusser, L. 1971. *Lenin and Philosophy and Other Essays.* Trans. B. Brewster. New York: Monthly Review Press.

Alvermann, D., ed. 2004. *Adolescents and Literacies in a Digital World.* New York: Peter Lang.

Alvermann, D., ed. 2010. *Adolescents' Online Literacies: Connecting Classrooms, Digital Media, and Popular Culture.* New York: Peter Lang.

Anderson, J., and V. Macleroy. 2016. *Multilingual Digital Storytelling: Engaging Creatively and Critically with Literacy.* New York: Routledge.

Anyon, J. 2009a. "Critical Pedagogy Is Not Enough: Social Justice Education, Political Participation, and the Politicization of Students." In *The Routledge International Handbook of Critical Education,* ed. M. Apple, W. Au, and L. Gandin, 389–95). New York: Routledge.

Anyon, J., ed. 2009b. *Theory and Educational Research: Toward Critical Social Explanation.* New York: Routledge.

Anzaldúa, G. 1987. *Borderlands/La Frontera: The New Mestiza.* San Francisco: Aunt Lute Books.

Appadurai, A. 1996. *Modernity at Large: Cultural Dimensions of Globalization.* Minneapolis: University of Minnesota Press.

Apple, M., W. Au, and L. Gandin, eds. 2009. *The Routledge International Handbook of Critical Education.* New York: Routledge.

Applebee, A., and J. Langer. 2013. *Writing Instruction That Works: Proven Methods for Middle and High School Classrooms.* Berkeley, Calif., and New York: National Writing Project and Teachers College Press.

Azano, A. 2011. "The Possibility of Place: One Teacher's Use of Place-Based Instruction for English Students in a Rural High School." *Journal of Research in Rural Education* 26, no. 10: 1–12.

Azano, A. (forthcoming). *Place to Learn: Place-Based Pedagogy and Critical Literacy.* New York: Bloomsbury.

Bakhtin, M. 1981. *The Dialogic Imagination.* Austin: University of Texas Press.

Ball, E., and A. Lai. 2006. "Place-Based Pedagogy for the Arts and Humanities." *Pedagogy: Critical Approaches to Teaching Literature, Language, Composition, and Culture* 6, no. 2: 261–87.

Banks, J., and C. Banks. 2010. *Multicultural Education: Issues and Perspectives.* Hoboken, N.J.: Wiley and Sons.

Barad, K. 2003. "Posthumanist Performativity: Toward an Understanding of How Matter Comes to Matter." *Signs: Journal of Women in Culture and Society* 28, no. 3: 801–31.

Barad, K. 2007. *Meeting the Universe Halfway: Quantum Physics and the Entanglement of Matter and Meaning.* Durham, N.C.: Duke University Press.

Barron, B. 2006. "Learning Ecologies for Technological Fluency: Gender and Experience Differences." *Journal of Educational Computing Research* 31, no. 1: 1–36.

Beach, R. 2007. *teachingmedialiteracy.com: A Web-Linked Guide to Resources and Activities.* New York: Teachers College Press.

Black, R. 2008. *Adolescents and Online Fan Fiction.* New York: Peter Lang.

Blommaert, J. 2008. *Grassroots Literacy: Writing, Identity, and Voice in Central Africa.* London: Routledge.

Bonilla, Y., and J. Rosa. 2015. "#Ferguson: Digital Protest, Hashtag Ethnography, and the Racial Politics of Social Media in the United States." *American Ethnologist* 42, no. 1: 4–17.

Bowers, C. A. 2008. "Why a Critical Pedagogy of Place Is an Oxymoron." *Environmental Education Research* 14, no. 3: 325–35.

boyd, d. 2014. *It's Complicated: The Social Lives of Networked Teens.* New Haven, Conn.: Yale University Press.

Brandt, D., and K. Clinton. 2002. "Limits of the Local: Expanding Perspectives on Literacy as a Social Practice." *Journal of Literacy Research* 34, 337–76.

Braynham, M., and M. Prinsloo, eds. 2009. *Literacies, Global and Local.* Amsterdam: John Benjamins Publishing.

Bronfenbrenner, U. 1994. "Ecological Models of Human Development." In *International Encyclopedia of Education Volume 3*, 2nd ed., ed. T. Husen and T. N. Postlethwaite, 1643–47. Oxford: Pergamon.

Bruce, B., A. P. Bishop, and N. R. Budhathoki, eds. 2014. *Youth Community Inquiry: New Media for Community and Personal Growth.* New York: Peter Lang.

Bruce, D. 2009. "Writing with Visual Images: Examining the Video Composition Processes of High School Students." *Research in the Teaching of English* 43, no. 4: 426–50.

Bruner, J. 1991. "The Narrative Construction of Reality." *Critical Inquiry* 18, 1–21.

Buckingham, D., ed. 2006. *Youth, Identity, and Digital Media.* Cambridge, Mass.: MIT Press.

Burn, A. 2009. *Making New Media: Creative Production and Digital Literacies.* New York: Peter Lang.

Burwell, C. 2010. "Rewriting the Script: Toward a Politics of Young People's Digital Media Participation." *Review of Education, Pedagogy, and Cultural Studies* 32, no. 4–5: 382–402.

Carspecken, P. 1996. *Critical Ethnography in Educational Research: A Theoretical and Practical Guide.* New York: Routledge.

Casey, E., ed. 2009. *Getting Back into Place: Toward a Renewed Understanding of the Place-World.* London: Routledge.

Center for Social Media. 2007. *The Cost of Copyright Confusion for Media Literacy.* Washington, D.C.: American University.

Chang, J. 2005. *Can't Stop Won't Stop: A History of the Hip-Hop Generation.* New York: St. Martin's Press.

Charmaraman, L. 2008. "Media Gangs of Social Resistance: Urban Adolescents Take Back Their Images and Their Streets through Media Production." *After School Matters* 7: 23–33. http://www.niost.org/pdf/afterschoolmatters/asm_2008_7_spring/asm_2008_7_spring-3.pdf.

Chisholm, J., and B. Trent, 2014. "Digital Storytelling in a Place-Based Composition Course." *Journal of Adolescent and Adult Literacy* 57, no. 4: 307–18.

Cobb, P., J. Confrey, A. diSessa, R. Lehrer, and L. Schauble. 2003. "Design Experiments in Educational Research." *Educational Researcher* 32, no. 1: 9–13.

Cochran-Smith, M., and S. Lytle. 1993. *Inside/Outside: Teacher Research and Knowledge.* New York: Teachers College Press.

Cochran-Smith, M., and S. Lytle. 1999. "The Teacher Research Movement: A Decade Later." *Educational Researcher* 28, no. 7: 15–25.

Cohen, K., J. Kahne, B. Bowyer, E. Middaugh, and J. Rogowski. 2012. *Participatory Politics: New Media and Youth Political Action.* Oakland, Calif.: YPP Network/MacArthur Foundation.

Coiro, J., M. Knobel, C. Lankshear, and D. Leu, eds. 2008. *Handbook of Research on New Literacies.* New York: Routledge.

Comber, B. 2011. "Making Space for Place-Making Pedagogies: Stretching Normative Mandated Literacy Curriculum." *Contemporary Issues in Early Childhood* 12, no. 4: 343–48.

Comber, B. 2013. "Schools as Meeting Places: Critical and Inclusive Literacies in Changing Local Environments." *Language Arts* 90, no. 5: 361–71.

Comber, B., and H. Nixon. 2013. "Urban Renewal, Migration, and Memories: The Affordances of Place-Based Pedagogies for Developing Immigrant Students' Literate Repertoires." *Multidisciplinary Journal of Educational Research* 3, no. 1: 42–68.

Comber, B., H. Nixon, L. Ashmore, S. Loo, and J. Cook. 2006. "Urban Renewal from the Inside Out: Spatial and Critical Literacies in a Low Socioeconomic School Community." *Mind, Culture, and Activity* 13, no. 3: 228–46.

Comber, B., H. Nixon, and J. Reid, eds. 2007. *Literacies in Place: Teaching Environmental Communications.* Newtown, New South Wales, Australia: Primary English Teaching Association.

Coole, D., and S. Frost, eds. 2010. *New Materialisms: Ontology, Agency, and Politics.* Durham, N.C.: Duke University Press.

Coryat, D., and S. Goodman. 2004. *Developing the Youth Media Field: Perspectives from Two Practitioners.* New York: Open Society Institute.

Creswell, T. 2004. *Place: An Introduction.* Malden, Mass.: Wiley.

Davies, J., and G. Merchant. 2009. *Web 2.0 for Schools: Learning and Social Participation.* New York: Peter Lang.

de Certeau, M. 1984. *The Practice of Everyday Life*. Berkeley: University of California Press.

Deleuze, G., and F. Guattari.1987. *A Thousand Plateaus: Capitalism and Schizophrenia*. Trans. B. Massumi. Minneapolis: University of Minnesota Press.

Delwiche, A., and J. J. Henderson, eds. 2013. *The Participatory Cultures Handbook*. New York: Routledge.

Denzin, N. 2001. *Interpretive Interactionism*. 2nd ed. Thousand Oaks, Calif.: Sage.

Denzin, N. 2003. *Performance Ethnography: Critical Pedagogy and the Politics of Culture*. Thousand Oaks, Calif.: Sage.

Denzin, N. 2014. *Interpretive Autobiography*. Thousand Oaks, Calif.: Sage.

Digital Media and Learning Research Hub. 2012. *Connected Learning*. https://dmlhub.net/publications/connected-learning-agenda-for-research-and-design/

Dimitriadis, G. 2001. *Performing Identity/Performing Culture: Hip Hop as Text, Pedagogy, and Lived Practice*. New York: Peter Lang.

Dyson, A. H. 2003. *The Brothers and Sisters Learn to Write: Popular Literacies in Childhood and School Cultures*. New York: Teachers College Press.

Emdin, C. 2010. *Science Urban Education for the Hip-Hop Generation*. Rotterdam, Netherlands: Sense.

Fairclough, N. 1989. *Language and Power*. London: Longman.

Feldman, A. 1998. "Implementing and Assessing the Power of Conversation in the Teaching of Action Research." *Teacher Education Quarterly* 25, no. 2: 27–42.

Ferguson, R. 2001. "Media Education and the Development of Critical Solidarity." *Media Education Journal* 30, 37–43.

Fine, M. 1994. "Working the Hyphens: Reinventing Self and Other in Qualitative Research." In N. Denzin and Y. Lincoln, eds., *Handbook of Qualitative Research*, 70–82. Thousand Oaks, Calif.: Sage.

Fisher, M. T. 2007. *Writing in Rhythm: Spoken Word in Urban Classrooms*. New York: Teachers College Press.

Fisher, M. T. 2009. *Black Literate Lives: Historical and Contemporary Perspectives*. New York: Routledge.

Fisherkeller, J., ed. 2011. *International Perspectives on Youth Media: Cultures of Production and Education*. New York: Peter Lang.

Foucault, M. 1977. *Discipline and Punish*. Trans. A. Sheridan. New York: Vintage.

Friedel, T. L. 2011. "Looking for Learning in All the Wrong Places: Urban Native Youth's Cultured Response to Western-Oriented Place-Based Learning." *International Journal of Qualitative Studies in Education* 24, no. 5: 531–46.

Gay, G. 2010. *Culturally Responsive Teaching: Theory, Research, and Practice*. New York: Teachers College Press.

Gee, J. 2003. *What Video Games Have to Teach Us about Learning and Literacy*. New York: Palgrave Macmillan.

Gee, J. 2007. *Good Video Games and Good Learning: Collected Essays on Video Games, Learning and Literacy*. New York: Peter Lang.

Giroux, H. 2004. "Cultural Studies, Public Pedagogy, and the Responsibility of Intellectuals." *Communication and Critical/Cultural Studies* 1, no. 1: 59–79.

Giroux, H. 2012. *Disposable Youth, Racialized Memories, and the Culture of Cruelty*. New York: Routledge.

Giroux, H., and R. Simon, eds. 1989. *Popular Culture, Schooling, and Everyday Life.* Toronto: Ontario Institute for Studies in Education Press.

Glaeser, E., and J. Vigdor. 2012. *The End of the Segregated Century: Racial Separation in America's Neighborhoods, 1890–2010.* New York: Manhattan Institute for Policy Research. https://www.manhattan-institute.org/pdf/cr_66.pdf.

Glaser, B., and A. Strauss. 1967. *The Discovery of Grounded Theory: Strategies for Qualitative Research.* Chicago, Ill.: Aldine.

Goodman, S. 2003. *Teaching Youth Media: A Critical Guide to Literacy, Video Production, and Social Change.* New York: Teachers College Press.

Graham, M. 2007. "Art, Ecology, and Art Education: Locating Art Education in a Critical Place-Based Pedagogy." *Studies in Art Education: A Journal of Issues and Research* 48, no. 4: 375–91.

Gruenewald, D. 2003a. "Foundations of Place: A Multidisciplinary Framework for Place-Conscious Education." *American Educational Research Journal* 40, no. 3: 619–54.

Gruenewald, D. 2003b. "The Best of Both Worlds: A Critical Pedagogy of Place." *Educational Researcher* 32, no. 4: 3–12.

Gruenewald, D. 2008. "Place-Based Education: Grounding Culturally Responsive Teaching in Geographical Diversity." In D. Gruenewald and G. Smith, eds. *Place-Based Education in the Global Age.* New York: Lawrence Erlbaum.

Gutiérrez, K., and A. Arzubiaga. 2012. "An Ecological and Activity Theoretic Approach to Studying Diasporic and Nondominant Communities." In *Research on Schools, Neighborhoods, and Communities: Toward Civic Responsibility,* ed. W. Tate, 203–16. Lanham, N.Y.: Rowman and Littlefield.

Gutiérrez, K. G., and B. Rogoff. 2003. "Cultural Ways of Learning: Individual Traits or Repertoires of Practice." *Educational Researcher* 32, no. 5: 19–25.

Guzzetti, B., K. Elliott, and D. Welsch. 2010. *DIY Media in the Classroom: New Literacies across Content Areas.* New York: Teachers College Press.

Hall, S. 1992: "Encoding/Decoding." In *Culture, Media, Language,* ed. S. Hall, D. Hobson, A. Lowe, and P. Willis, 128–38. London: Routledge/Center for Contemporary Cultural Studies.

Hall, S., ed. 1997. *Representation: Cultural Representation and Signifying Practices.* London: Sage.

Halverson, E. 2010. "Film as Identity Exploration: A Multimodal Analysis of Youth-Produced Films." *Teachers College Record* 112, no. 9: 2352–78.

Hill, M. L. 2009. *Beats, Rhymes, and Classroom Life: Hip-Hop Pedagogy and the Politics of Identity.* New York: Teachers College Press.

Hill, M. L., and L. Vasudevan, eds. 2009. *Media, Learning, and Sites of Possibility.* New York: Peter Lang.

Hobbs, R. 2007. *Reading the Media: Media Literacy in High School English.* New York: Teachers College Press.

Hobbs, R. 2011. *Digital and Media Literacy: Connecting Culture and Classroom.* Thousand Oaks, Calif.: Corwin/Sage.

Hobbs, R., and Donnelly, K. 2011. "Toward a Pedagogy of Fair Use for Multimedia Composition." In *Copy(write): Intellectual Property in the Writing Classroom,* ed. M. Rife, S. Slattery, and D. DeVoss, 275–94. West Lafayette, Ind.: Parlor Press.

Hodge, R., and, G. Kress. 1988. *Social Semiotics*. Cambridge, U.K.: Polity.

Hull, G., and M. Katz. 2006. "Crafting an Agentive Self: Case Studies of Digital Storytelling." *Research in the Teaching of English* 41, 43–81.

Hull, G., and M. Nelson. 2005. "Locating the Semiotic Power of Multimodality." *Written Communication* 22, no. 2: 224–61.

Hull, G., and K. Schultz, eds. 2002. *School's Out! Bridging Out-of-School Literacies with Classroom Practice*. New York: Teachers College Press.

Ingalis, R. 2012. "'Stealing the Air': The Poet-Citizens of Youth Spoken-Word." *Journal of Popular Culture* 45, no. 1: 99–117.

Ito, M. 2010. *Hanging Out, Messing Around, and Geeking Out: Kids Living and Learning with New Media*. Cambridge, Mass.: MIT Press.

Ito, M., K. Gutiérrez, S. Livingstone, B. Penuel, J. Rhodes, K. Salen, J. Schor, J. Sefton-Green, and S. C. Watkins. 2013. *Connected Learning: An Agenda for Research and Design*. Irvine, Calif.: Digital Media and Learning Research Hub.

Ito, M., E. Soep, N. Kliger-Vilenchik, S. Shresthova, L. Gamber-Thompson, and A. Zimmerman. 2015. "Learning Connected Civics: Narratives, Practices, Infrastructures." *Curriculum Inquiry* 45, no. 1: 10–29.

Jackson, A., and L. Mazzei. 2012. *Thinking with Theory in Qualitative Research: Viewing Data across Multiple Perspectives*. New York: Routledge.

Janks, H. 2010. *Literacy and Power*. New York: Routledge.

Jenkins, H. 2006a. *Confronting the Challenges of Participatory Culture: Media Education for the 21st Century*. Chicago: MacArthur Foundation.

Jenkins, H. 2006b. *Convergence Culture: Where Old and New Media Collide*. New York: New York University Press.

Jenkins, H., M. Ito, and d. boyd. 2016. *Participatory Culture in a Networked Era: A Conversation on Youth, Learning, Commerce, and Politics*. Malden, Mass.: Polity.

Jocson, K. M. 2008. *Youth Poets: Empowering Literacies In and Out of Schools*. New York: Peter Lang.

Jocson, K. M. 2010. "Unpacking Symbolic Creativities: Writing in School and across Contexts." *Review of Education, Pedagogy, and Cultural Studies* 32, no. 2: 206–36.

Jocson, K. M. 2012. "Youth Media as Narrative Assemblage: Examining New Literacies at an Urban High School." *Pedagogies: An International Journal* 7, no. 4: 298–316.

Jocson, K. M. 2013a. "Remix Revisited: Critical Solidarity in Youth Media Arts." *E-Learning and Digital Media* 10, no. 1: 68–82.

Jocson, K. M., ed. 2013b. *Cultural Transformations: Youth and Pedagogies of Possibility*. Cambridge, Mass.: Harvard Education Press.

Jocson, K. M. 2015a. "New Media Literacies as Social Action: The Centrality of Pedagogy in the Politics of Knowledge Production." *Curriculum Inquiry* 45, no. 1: 30–51.

Jocson, K. M. 2015b. "'I Want to Do More and Change Things': Reframing CTE toward Possibilities in Urban Education." *Urban Education*. doi: 10.1177/0042085915618714.

Jocson, K. M. 2016a. "'Put Us on the Map': Place-Based Media Production and Critical Inquiry in CTE." *International Journal of Qualitative Studies Education* 29, no. 10: 1269–86.

Jocson, K. M. 2016b. "Digital Storytelling: Using Producer's Commentary in the Classroom." *Transformations: The Journal of Inclusive Scholarship and Pedagogy* 26, no. 1: 106–13.

Jocson, K. M. 2016c. "Ripples and Breaks: Reflection on Learning Ecologies in Career and Technical Education." *Anthropology and Education Quarterly* 47, no. 4: 444–55.

Jocson, K. M., with A. Carpenter. 2016. "Translocal Assemblage and the Practice of Alternative Media toward Racial Justice: A Pedagogical Perspective." *Critical Studies in Education.* doi: 10.1080/17508487.2016.1234493.

Jocson, K. M., with E. Jacobs-Fantauzzi. 2013. "'Barely Audible': A Remix of Poetry and Video as Pedagogical Practice." In *Cultural Transformations: Youth and Pedagogies of Possibility,* ed. K. M. Jocson, 13–31. Cambridge, Mass.: Harvard Education Press.

Jocson, K. M., and J. Rosa. 2015. "Rethinking Gaps: Literacies and Languages in Participatory Cultures." *Journal of Adult and Adolescent Literacy* 58, no. 5: 372–74.

Jocson, K. M., and J. Share. 2012. "From New Media to Critical Media Literacies: Politics, Practice, and Pedagogy." In *International Handbook of Teacher and School Development,* ed. C. Day, 351–59. London: Routledge.

Jocson, K. M., and E. Thorne-Wallington. 2013. "Mapping Literacy Rich Environments: Geospatial Perspectives on Literacy and Education." *Teachers College Record* 115, no. 6: 1–24.

Joseph, M. B., and B. Cook. 2013. "Life Is Living: An Arts Festival Focused on Healing, Community Collaboration, and the Creative Ecosystem." In *Cultural Transformations: Youth and Pedagogies of Possibility,* ed. K. M. Jocson, 33–51. Cambridge, Mass.: Harvard Education Press.

Kafai, Y., and K. Peppler. 2011. "Youth, Technology, and DIY: Developing Participatory Competencies in Creative Media Production." In "Youth Cultures, Language, and Literacy," ed. S. Wortham, *Review of Research in Education* 35, 89–119.

Kellner, D. 1995. *Media Culture: Cultural Studies, Identity, and Politics Between the Modern and the Postmodern.* New York: Routledge.

Kellner, D., and G. Kim. 2010. "YouTube, Critical Pedagogy, and Media Activism." *Review of Education, Pedagogy, and Cultural Studies* 32, no. 1: 3–36.

Kellner, D., and J. Share. 2005. "Toward Critical Media Literacy: Core Concepts, Debates, Organizations, and Policy." *Discourse: Studies in the Cultural Politics of Education* 26, no. 3: 369–86.

Kellner, D., and J. Share. 2007. "Critical Media Literacy Is Not an Option." *Learning Inquiry* 1, no. 1: 59–69.

Kinloch, V. 2009. *Harlem on Our Minds: Place, Race, and Literacies of Urban Youth.* New York: Teachers College Press.

Kist, W. 2005. *New Literacies in Action: Teaching and Learning in Multiple Media.* New York: Teachers College Press.

Kitwana, B. 2002. *The Hip Hop Generation: Young Blacks and the Crisis in African-American Culture.* New York: Basic Books.

Knobel, M., and C. Lankshear, eds. 2010. *DIY Media.* New York: Peter Lang.

Kress, G. 2001. "Multimodality." In *Multiliteracies: Literacy Learning and the Design of Social Futures,* ed. B. Cope and M. Kalantzis, 182–202. London: Routledge.

Kress, G. 2003. *Literacy in the New Media Age.* London: Routledge.

Kress, G., and T. Van Leeuwen. 2001. *Multimodal Discourse: The Modes and Media of Contemporary Communication.* London: Arnold.

Kuttner, P. 2015. "Educating for Cultural Citizenship: Reframing the Goals of Arts Education." *Curriculum Inquiry* 45, no. 1: 69–92.

Labov, W., and J. Waletzky. 1967. "Narrative Analysis." In *Essays on the Verbal and Visual Arts,* ed. J. Helm, 12–44. Seattle: University of Washington Press.

Lam, W. S. A. 2009. "Multiliteracies on Instant Messaging in Negotiating Local, Translocal, and Transnational Affiliations: A Case of an Adolescent Immigrant." *Reading Research Quarterly* 44, no. 4: 377–97.

Lankshear, C., and M. Knobel. 2006. *New Literacies: Everyday Practices and Classroom Learning,* 2nd ed. Berkshire, U.K.: Open University Press.

Latour, B. 2005. *Reassembling the Social: An Introduction to Actor-Network-Theory.* New York: Oxford University Press.

Leander, K., N. Phillips, and K. Taylor. 2010. "The Changing Social Spaces of Learning: Mapping New Mobilities." *Review of Research in Education* 34, no.1: 329–94.

Lee, C. D. 2007. *Culture, Literacy, and Learning: Taking Bloom in the Midst of the Whirlwind.* New York: Teachers College Press.

Lee, C. D. 2010. "Soaring above the Clouds, Delving the Ocean's Depths: Understanding the Ecologies of Human Learning and the Challenge for Education Science." *Educational Researcher* 39, no. 9: 643–55.

Lefebvre, H. 1991 (1974). *The Production of Space.* D. Nicholson-Smith, trans. Oxford, U.K.: Blackwell.

Leonardo, Z., and R. Allen. 2008. "On Ideology: An Overview." In *The SAGE Encyclopedia of Qualitative Research Methods,* ed. L. Given, 415–20. Thousand Oaks, Calif.: Sage.

Lesley, M., and M. Matthews. 2009. "Place-Based Essay Writing and Content Area Literacy Instruction for Preservice Secondary Teachers." *Journal of Adolescent and Adult Literacy* 52, no. 6: 523–33.

Lessig, L. 2008. *Remix: Making Art and Commerce Thrive in a Hybrid Economy.* New York: Penguin.

Leu, D. J., Jr., and C. K. Kinzer. 2000. "The Convergence of Literacy Instruction and Networked Technologies for Information and Communication." *Reading Research Quarterly* 35, 108–27.

Leu, D. J., Jr., I. O'Byrne, L. Zawilinski, G. McVerry, and H. Everett-Cacopardo. 2009. "Expanding the New Literacies Conversation." *Educational Researcher* 38, no. 4: 264–69.

Levi-Strauss, C. 1966. *The Savage Mind.* Chicago: University of Chicago Press.

Lévy, P. 1997. *Collective Intelligence: Mankind's Emerging World in Cyberspace.* Cambridge, Mass.: Perseus.

Lievrouw, L. 2011. *Alternative and Activist New Media.* Malden, Mass.: Polity.

Lister, M., J. Dovey, S. Giddings, I. Grant, and K. Kelly. 2009. *New Media: A Critical Introduction.* 2nd ed. New York: Routledge.

Lorde, A. 1978. *The Black Unicorn.* New York: Norton.

Love, B. 2012. *Hip Hop's Li'l Sistas Speak: Negotiating Hip Hop Identities and Politics in the New South.* New York: Peter Lang.

Luke, A., A. Woods, and K. Weir, eds. 2013. *Curriculum, Syllabus Design, and Equity: A Primer and Model*. New York: Routledge.

Madison, S. 2005. *Critical Ethnography: Method, Ethics, and Performance*. Thousand Oaks, Calif.: Sage.

Mahiri, J. 2006. "Digital DJ-ing: Rhythms of Learning in an Urban School." *Language Arts* 84, no. 1: 55–61.

Maira, S., and E. Soep, eds. *Youthscapes: The Popular, the National, the Global*. Philadelphia: University of Pennsylvania Press.

Manovich, L. 2000. *The Language of New Media*. Cambridge, Mass.: MIT Press.

Massey, D. 1984. *Spatial Divisions of Labour*. Basingstoke, U.K.: Macmillan.

Massey, D. 1994. *Space, Place, and Gender*. Minneapolis: University of Minnesota Press.

Massey, D. 2005. *For Space*. London: Sage.

Masterman, L. 1990. *Teaching the Media*. New York: Routledge.

Matias, C., and T. Grosland. 2016. "Digital Storytelling as Racial Justice: Digital Hopes for Deconstructing Whiteness in Teacher Education." *Journal of Teacher Education* 67, no. 2: 152–64.

McFarlane, C. 2009. "Translocal Assemblages: Space, Power, and Social Movements." *Geoforum* 40, no. 4: 561–67.

McFarlane, C. 2012. *Learning the City: Knowledge and Translocal Assemblage*. West Sussex, U.K.: Wiley-Blackwell.

McInerney, P., J. Smyth, and B. Down. 2011. "'Coming to a Place Near You?' The Politics and Possibilities of a Critical Pedagogy of Place-Based Education." *Asia-Pacific Journal of Teacher Education* 39, no. 1: 3–16.

McIntyre. 2008. *Participatory Action Research*. Thousand Oaks, Calif.: Sage.

Media That Matters Film Festival. 2007. http://mediathatmattersfest-org.reel -lives.org/films/slip_of_the_tongue.

Medina, C. 2010. "Reading Across Communities." In *Biliteracy Practices: Examining Translocal Discourses and Cultural Flows in Literature. Reading Research Quarterly* 45, no. 1: 40–60.

Medina, C., and K. Wohlwend. 2014. *Literacy, Play, and Globalization: Converging Imaginaries in Children's Critical and Cultural Performances*. New York: Routledge.

Mihailidis, P. 2014. *Media Literacy and the Emerging Citizen: Youth, Engagement, and Participation in Digital Culture*. New York: Peter Lang.

Miller, P. 2004. *Rhythm Science*. Cambridge, Mass.: Mediawork/ MIT Press.

Missouri Department of Elementary and Secondary Education. 2011. *School Report Card*. http://mcds.dese.mo.gov.

Moje, E. 2002. "But Where Are the Youth? On the Value of Integrating Youth Culture into Literacy Theory." *Educational Theory* 52, no. 1: 97–120.

Moje, E. 2009. "A Call for New Research on New and Multi-Literacies." *Research in the Teaching of English* 43, no. 4: 348–62.

Morrell, E. 2004. *Linking Literacy and Popular Culture: Finding Connections for Lifelong Learning*. Norwood, Mass.: Christopher-Gordon.

Morrell, E. 2008. *Critical Literacy and Urban Youth: Pedagogies of Access, Dissent, and Liberation*. New York: Routledge.

Morrell, E., R. Dueñas, V. Garcia, and J. López. 2013. *Critical Media Pedagogy: Teaching for Achievement in City Schools*. New York: Teachers College Press.

Morrell, E., and J. M. Duncan-Andrade. 2002. "Promoting Academic Literacy with Urban Youth through Engaging Hip-Hop Culture." *English Journal* 91, no. 6: 88–92.

National Alliance for Media Arts and Culture. 2003. *A Closer Look 2003: Case Studies from NAMAC's Youth Media Initiative.* San Francisco: NAMAC.

Nespor, J. 2008. "Education and Place: A Review Essay." *Educational Theory* 58, no. 4: 475–89.

New London Group. 1996. "A Pedagogy of Multiliteracies: Designing Social Futures." *Harvard Educational Review* 66, no. 1: 60–92.

Nieto, S. 2002. *Language, Culture, and Teaching: Critical Perspectives for a New Century.* Mahwah, N.J.: Lawrence Erlbaum.

Nieto, S., and P. Bode. 2012. *Affirming Diversity: The Sociopolitical Context of Multicultural Education.* 6th ed. Boston: Pearson.

Noblit, G., S. Flores, and E. Murillo, eds. 2004. *Postcritical Ethnography: An Introduction.* Cresskill, N.J.: Hampton.

Ohler, J. 2013. *Digital Storytelling in the Classroom: New Media Pathways to Literacy, Learning, and Creativity.* 2nd ed. Thousand Oaks, Calif.: Corwin/Sage.

Osgerby, B. 2004. *Youth Media.* London: Routledge.

Palfrey, J., and U. Gasser. 2008. *Born Digital: Understanding the First Generation of Digital Natives.* New York: Penguin/Basic Books.

Paris, D., and M. Winn, eds. 2014. *Humanizing Research: Decolonizing Qualitative Inquiry with Youth and Communities.* Thousand Oaks, Calif.: Sage.

Patel, L. 2013. *Youth Held at the Border: Immigration, Education, and the Politics of Inclusion.* New York: Teachers College Press.

Patel, L. 2016. *Decolonizing Educational Research: From Ownership to Answerability.* New York: Routledge.

Peppler, K. 2010. "Media Arts: Arts Education for a Digital Age." *Teachers College Record* 112, no. 8: 2118–53.

Peppler, K. 2014. *New Creativity Paradigms: Arts Learning in the Digital Age.* New York: Peter Lang.

Pew Research Center. 2010. *Millennials: A Portrait of Generation Next.* Washington, D.C.: Pew Research Center.

Philip, T., and A. Garcia. 2013. "The Importance of Still Teaching the iGeneration: New Technologies and the Centrality of Pedagogy." *Harvard Educational Review* 83, no. 2: 300–319.

Pinkard, N., and K. Austin. 2011. "Digital Youth Network: Creating New Media Citizens through the Affinity Learning Model." *International Journal of Learning and Media* 2, no. 4.

Polkinghorne, D. 1988. *Narrative Knowing and the Human Sciences.* New York: State University of New York Press.

Potter, J. 2012. *Digital Media and Learner Identity: The New Curatorship.* New York: Palgrave Macmillan.

Ratto, M., and M. Boler, eds. 2014. *DIY Citizenship: Critical Media Making and Social Media.* Cambridge, Mass.: MIT Press.

Richardson, E. 2006. *Hiphop Literacies.* New York: Routledge.

Richmond, M., C. Robinson, and M. Sachs-Israel. 2008. *The Global Literacy Chal-*

lenge: A Profile of Youth and Adult Literacy at the Mid-point of the United Nations Literacy Decade 2003–2012. Paris: UNESCO.

Rideout, V., U. Foehr, and D. Roberts. 2010. Generation M2: Media in the Lives of 8–18 Year Olds. Menlo Park, Calif.: Kaiser Family Foundation.

Robin, B. 2008. "Digital Storytelling: A Powerful Technology Tool for the 21st Century Classroom." Theory Into Practice 47, no. 3: 220–28.

Rogers, T., K. L. Winters, A. M. LaMonde, and M. Perry. 2010. "From Image to Ideology: Analysing Shifting Identity Positions of Marginalized Youth across the Cultural Sites of Video Production." Pedagogies: An International Journal 5, no. 4: 298–312.

Rogers, T., K. L. Winters, M. Perry, and A. M. LaMonde. 2015. Youth, Critical Literacies, and Civic Engagement: Arts, Media, and Literacy in the Lives of Adolescents. New York: Routledge.

Rose, G. 2007. Visual Methodologies: An Introduction to the Interpretation of Visual Materials. Thousand Oaks, Calif.: Sage.

Rose, M. 2004. Mind at Work: Valuing the Intelligence of the American Worker. New York: Penguin.

Rose, M. 2012. "Rethinking Remedial Education and the Academic–Vocational Divide." Mind, Culture, and Activity 19, no. 1: 1–16.

Rose, M. 2014. "Reframing Career and Technical Education." Education Week, April 25, 2014. http://www.edweek.org/ew/articles/2014/04/25/30rose.h33.html.

Rose, T. 1994. Black Noise: Rap Music and Black Culture in Contemporary America. Hanover: Wesleyan.

Sanford, K., T. Rogers, and M. Kendrick. 2014. Everyday Youth Literacies: Critical Perspectives for New Times. Singapore: Springer.

Schneider, S., and K. Foot. 2005. "Web Sphere Analysis: An Approach to Studying Online Action." In Virtual Methods: Issues in Social Science Research on the Internet, ed. C. Hine, 157–70. Oxford, U.K.: Berg.

Scott, K., and M. White. 2011. "COMPUGIRLS' Standpoint: Culturally Responsive Computing and Its Effect on Girls of Color." Urban Education 48, no. 5: 657–81.

Seitz, W. 1961. The Art of Assemblage. New York: Doubleday.

Share, J. 2009. Media Literacy Is Elementary: Teaching Youth to Critically Read and Create Media. New York: Peter Lang.

Simpson, A. 2007. "On Ethnographic Refusal: Indigeneity, 'Voice,' and Colonial Citizenship." Junctures 9: 67–80.

Smith, G., and D. Gruenewald, eds. 2008. Place-Based Education in the Global Age: Local Diversity. New York: Routledge.

Smith, L. T. 1999. Decolonizing Methodologies: Research and Indigenous Peoples. New York: Zed.

Soep, E. 2011. "Youth Media Goes Mobile." National Civic Review 100, no. 3: 8–11. doi: 10.1002/ncr.20073.

Soep, E. 2014. Participatory Politics: Next-Generation Tactics to Remake Public Spheres. Cambridge, Mass.: MIT Press.

Soep, E., and V. Chávez. 2010. Drop That Knowledge: Youth Radio Stories. Berkeley: University of California Press.

Soja, E. 1989. Postmodern Geographies: The Reassertion of Space in Critical Social Theory. London: Verso.

Soja, E. 2010. *Seeking Spatial Justice*. Minneapolis: University of Minnesota Press.

Stovall, D. 2006a. "Urban Poetics: Poetry, Social Justice, and Critical Pedagogy in Education." *Urban Review* 38, no. 1: 63–80.

Stovall, D. 2006b. "We Can Relate: Hip-Hop Culture, Critical Pedagogy, and the Secondary Classroom." *Urban Education* 41, no. 6: 585–602.

Strauss, A., and J. Corbin.1998. *Basics of Qualitative Research: Techniques and Procedures for Developing Grounded Theory*. Thousand Oaks, Calif.: Sage.

Street, B. 1984. *Literacy in Theory and Practice*. Cambridge, U.K.: Cambridge University Press.

Street, B. 1995. *Social Literacies: Critical Approaches to Literacy in Development, Ethnography, and Education*. London: Longman.

Street, B. 2003. "What's New in New Literacy Studies?" *Current Issues in Comparative Education* 5, no. 2: 1–14.

Taylor, K.-Y. 2016. *From #Blacklivesmatter to Black Liberation*. Chicago: Haymarket.

Theobald, P. 1997. *Teaching the Commons: Place, Pride, and the Renewal of Community*. Boulder, Colo.: Westview.

Thomas, J. 1993. *Doing Critical Ethnography*. Newbury Park, Calif.: Sage.

Tinson, C., and C. McBride. 2013. "Hip Hop, Critical Pedagogy, and Radical Education in a Time of Crisis." *Radical Teacher* 97: 1–9.

Tuck, E. 2009. "Suspending Damage: A Letter to Communities." *Harvard Educational Review* 79, no. 3: 409–27.

Tuck, E., and M. McKenzie. 2015. *Place in Research: Theory, Methodology, and Methods*. New York: Routledge.

Tuck E., and K. W. Yang, eds. 2014. *Youth Resistance Research and Theories of Change*. New York: Routledge.

U.S. Department of Education. 2008. *Career and Technical Education in the United States: 1990 to 2005*. Washington, D.C.: U.S. Department of Education, Institute of Education Sciences, National Center for Education Statistics.

U.S. Department of Education. 2012. *Investing in America's Future: A Blueprint for Transforming Career and Technical Education*. Washington, D.C.: U.S. Department of Education, Office of Vocational and Adult Education.

Vasquez, V. 2004. *Negotiating Critical Literacies with Young Children*. Mahwah, N.J.: Lawrence Erlbaum.

Vasudevan, L. 2010. "Education Remix: New Media, Literacies, and the Emerging Digital Geographies." *Digital Culture and Education* 2, no. 1: 62–82.

Vasudevan, L., and T. DeJaynes. 2013. "Becoming 'Not Yet': Adolescents Making and Remaking Themselves in Art-Full Spaces." In *Arts, Media, and Justice: Multimodal Explorations with Youth*, ed. L. Vasudevan and T. DeJaynes, 1–26. New York: Peter Lang.

Vasudevan, L., and T. DeJaynes, eds. 2014. *Arts, Media, and Justice: Multimodal Explorations with Youth*. New York: Peter Lang.

Voithofer, R. J. 2005. "Designing New Media Education Research: The Materiality of Data, Presentation, and Dissemination." *Educational Researcher* 34, no. 9: 3–14.

Vossoughi, S., P. Hooper, and M. Escudé. 2016. "Making Through the Lens of Culture and Power: Transformative Visions for Educational Equity." *Harvard Educational Review* 86, no. 2: 206–32.

Waldman, D. 1992. *Collage, Assemblage, and the Found Object*. New York: Abrams.

Watkins, S. C. 2012. "From Theory to Design: Exploring the Power and Potential of 'Connected Learning,' Part Two." Available at http://theyoungandthedigital .com/2012/10/09/from-theory-to-design-exploring-the-power-potential-of -connected-learning-part-2/.

Williams, B., and A. Zenger, eds. 2012. *New Media Literacies and Participatory Cultures across Borders.* New York: Routledge.

Winn, M. 2011. *Girl Time: Literacy, Justice, and the School-to-Prison Pipeline.* New York: Teachers College Press.

Wortham, S. 2011. "Youth Cultures and Education." In *Youth Cultures, Language, and Literacy. Review of Research in Education* vol. 35, ed. S. Wortham, vii–xi. Washington, D.C.: American Educational Research Association.

Yang, W. 2007. "Organizing MySpace: Youth Walkouts, Pleasure, Politics, and New Media." *Educational Foundations* 21, no. 1–2: 9–28.

Yang, K. W. 2012. "Kutiman: It's the Mother of All Funk Chords." In *Art and Social Justice Education: Culture as Commons,* ed. T. Quinn, J. Ploof, and L. Hochtritt, 11–13. New York: Routledge.

Youdell, D. 2011. *School Trouble: Identity, Power, and Politics in Education.* New York: Routledge.

Index

Korina M. Jocson is associate professor of education at the University of Massachusetts Amherst, author of *Youth Poets: Empowering Literacies In and Out of Schools,* and editor of *Cultural Transformations: Youth and Pedagogies of Possibility.* She is editor-in-chief of the journal *Equity and Excellence in Education.*